1

Building

A

Champion:

THE FUNDAMENTALS OF PLAYING TENNIS, COACHING, AND PARENTING A SUCCESSFUL ATHLETE

Authored By Dan McCain

Table of Contents

SECTION 3. Tactics and Strategy.

A Special Thanks to My Dad, who taught me that the game can bring more than winning into someone's life. You taught me how to play the game, teach the player and coach the person.

And a big thank you to Vitaly Gorin, who made me into the coach I am today as much as anyone, and who took the time to talk shop with me when Jose wasn't around, when it was a weekday, or a weekend, or at lunch time, or in the evening, or during lessons, and so on.

And I bow to Lee Hurst, who I learned more from and had more fun working with than just about anyone I've ever met.

I'd also like to thank my wife, Jenna, my Mom, and my sister Kelly, for believing in me.

Introduction

The term "the whole nine yards" came from World War Two fighter pilots in the South Pacific. When arming their airplanes on the ground, the .50 caliber machine gun ammo belts measured exactly twenty-seven feet, before being loaded into the fuselage. If the pilots fired all their ammo at a target, it got "the whole nine yards."

I've seen a lot of tennis books out there, and like anything else – some are pretty good, and most are not. When I shuffle through the shelves of the sports and tennis section in Barnes and Noble, I see books by past pros that discuss their journeys on the pro tour or how they helped this already established professional player or maybe even how they overcame their fear about winning.

What I've seen consistently though, is a lack of comprehensive information that provides a literal and visual "how to" when it comes to raising and building a champion. There are books on the mental game that lack stroke production material, and vice versa, but no one book serves as an all-encompassing bible that any coach or player can pick up when a question arises.

This isn't one of those either.

What this book provides you with is as wide a range of ideas about the game as possible. It attempts to offer "the whole nine yards" to you about the game of tennis.

This book provides as many ideas about the mental, emotional, and physical game as I can think of, and that people I trust know of. Unfortunately for me and fortunately for you, there aren't that many people that call themselves coaches that I trust. So the exchange of ideas here in this book comes filtered from many and put together by few.

There are elements in the book that discuss what it means to be a smart player in regards to tactics and strategy. There are chapters that describe technique for every shot in the book (in 2010), and chapters that describe as comprehensively as possible the footwork on each stroke in a range of situations. The book also attempts to create a philosophy about how one approaches the game that promotes not just what most coaches refer to as "mental toughness", but also fulfillment on the court regardless of outcome.

While the science of success and achievement are addressed in practical terms for players, parents, and coaches, the book also seeks to create a set of ideals regarding the art of fulfillment beyond winning and losing. After all, this is a game we're talking about, right?

This book is not just about child development. It's about human development. It's about building a champion from scratch – and then being able to motivate those champions to have a genuine desire to constantly get better. It's about teaching a player the perfect strokes for them, how to make the best decisions on their own on court, how to take care of their minds and bodies, and how to teach them to play with their hearts. It's about wanting to be really good at everything – and then doing it.

I don't see this game as really that complex when you get down to the root of it. Every stroke has basic concepts that, when they are not achieved, have a myriad of complex complications that take place as a result, depending on the person and the player. But within each stroke, a few certain things have to happen, and when they do not – that's when things get difficult.

It's like learning language – you know all the letters in the alphabet, right? There are 26 of them, and you know them all and how they are used in a range of situations, because there is only so much to know about the alphabet – there is a finite amount of information there for you to understand. It's limited in scope.

So is your forehand technique. How would you like to know everything about your forehand, literally? Sound good? Well, you can. There's only so much going on there.

Now how to use it – that's another story. That's when personal preference, offensive and defensive and neutral situations and court positioning and game style and strategic decision making against various opponents – all of that contributes to how a player can use their forehand, and for some al of those ideas swirling together can make someone's head spin. But even those parts can be reduced to a few simple ideas that can be expanded on. And that's a big part of this book – getting down to the root of the issue from each stroke or point play or strategy – and then branching out from there. It's about identifying the few key components from which everything stems from, and building from those foundations.

The same goes for personality and thought patterns on the court too. For every successful player, there are some common denominators of how these players think, how they operate within their body language, and how they look to strategically impose their will onto their opponents.

For the past 13 years, I've had hundreds of people come to me from all over the world each year with this problem with their forehand or that issue with their backhand or serve and so on. After a while the patterns exhibited by all these players and personalities begin to look pretty similar.

I get the phone call when someone has a tournament the next day and they've totally lost their minds and they can't hit their second serve and they're double faulting all over the place. Or when their last coach told them not to go practice with their friend, or promised them a better volley and it never happened.

It's the player on my college team complaining about this stroke during our last dual match, my young junior layer complaining about that particular stroke at nationals in Kalamazoo, my touring pro worrying about this particular opponent at his next challenger event, or even my adult concerned about returning his 4.0 league partner's serve.

And so on.

But the fact of the matter is that once these elements are identified, once these fundamentals are understood – the elements of technique, of strategy and tactics, or how to think and recognize your thought patterns – and in large part of just what it means to be a successful person – we too can reproduce them in our own ways and find satisfaction in how we perform.

We too can reach our potential. We too can see just how good we can be at this sport. But it requires good habits – and Chapter 1 should deluge you with a number of ideas that can expose the good and not so good habits that you may possess that perhaps contribute or detract from your ability to maximize your ability.

And for me – that's the great thing about teaching and coaching – which I distinguish, by the way (more on that later). I can always learn from my students, and they can always learn from me. It's an exchange of ideas for the benefit of us both, or us all in a group setting. The act of sharing ideas is the act of giving – and like Paul McCartney once said, "the more you give, the more you get".

*   *   *   *

In my life, the game of tennis has been good to me. I wasn't born with a racquet in my hand, but there are pictures all over my parents' house with tiny versions of me running around with a Jack Kramer wood racquet that appears to be longer than I was tall.

The game allowed me to spend more time with my family, paid for my higher education, and gave me job opportunities all over the country that I never otherwise would have had.

Both of my parents and my sister have been college coaches, so moving in that direction was natural for me after coaching on the pro tour and teaching at clubs and academies. But regardless of whom I have had the privilege to work with, coaching, it seems to me, has been about addressing the human condition.

Building champions is a lot like building a house. First comes the foundation, and then you build up from there, adding pieces as you go. It's a progressive construction of a player.

Building a champion on the court has everything to do allowing people to access their brilliant selves both on and off court, motivating people to evolve, developing the idealism about the game in others, and the constant perfection of fundamentals. All players are more than the sum of their parts, and only a holistic approach of body, mind, heart, and soul by a player and his or her coach will yield real results. Each player's ability to play with heart and passion, and their ability to let their personalities off the court shine through on the court have more to do with their success or lack thereof than their ability to articulate and execute technique, tactics, or strategy.

Anyone would be hard-pressed to say that Rafael Nadal has better mechanics and tactical prowess than virtually any of his competition, but somehow he gets the better of them most of the time. He is the Secretariat of our generation, a thoroughbred with a huge heart, unlimited determination, genuine belief in himself, and a man who establishes his confidence on tireless preparation and hard work.

Without question tennis is a game that mirrors our lives, and certainly how we behave on the court is a microcosm of our behavior off the court. With our inner and outer strength, our attention to detail, our desire to reach our peak performance, and our never-ending battle with our flaws and inner demons all being constantly exposed, the game of tennis is really a game of life.

Grand Slam Champion Virginia Wade once said, "It's difficult for most people to imagine the creative process in tennis. Seemingly it's just an athletic matter of hitting the ball consistently well within the boundaries of the court. That analysis is just as specious as thinking that the difficulty in portraying King Lear on stage is learning all the lines. "

The X's and O's of the game will be addressed in this book, as will the mental aspects of the game and how different types of thinking and being can affect one's capacity to implement these specific aspects of the game in matches. By taking a close look at each stroke and each typical situation we all experience during matches, we can begin to analyze not just what works, but why. Certainly we can learn from what the pros do, and by identifying, for example, the common denominators and similarities of some of the great forehands on tour, we can begin to learn more about how we can all benefit from applying these concepts to our own forehands. We can take their ideas and make them our own, and begin to understand why their forehands are so great, and discover that by executing the same simple elements of technique that they do – we too can have great forehands.

I've been lucky to be exposed to some very smart men and women in this game, most notably my father, David McCain, as well as other mentors like ATP Tour Coach and Russian Davis Cup Coach Vitaly Gorin – and let's not forget the legendary Jose Higueras, who coached Sampras and Federer and Courier and Chang and Capriati and Todd Martin and Sergi Bruguera and the list goes on and on. Working with former USTA National Coach and Tour Coach Lee Hurst has been a blessing for me and perhaps more profound in my coaching education than working with anyone. And standing next to a range top coaches during my time working for the USTA had a significant effect on my growth as a coach as well. Growing up at

Saddlebrook tennis academy in Tampa can do things for your standards of operation within the game by exposing you to a wide ray of brilliant people right and left as well.

This book shares my experiences with you while passing much of what I have learned over the years, as a player and a coach. While I had some success as a player, being a ranked in the top 20 in the country as a junior and playing at the University of Michigan, I consider my career as a coach far more substantial –mainly because it's been far more rewarding. It's like Nick Nolte's character said in *Way of the Peaceful Warrior* –"Service to others - there's no higher calling."

So whether or not you are an aspiring, soon-to-be champion, or a coach who is fixed on building champions, there are different parts of this book that can benefit you. Maybe none of it will, or maybe it all will, but regardless of your level, we can all become better players and better coaches, and we can all more specifically define how to execute or teach the mental and physical fundamentals of this game.

Section 1. Environment

Chapter 1.

The Collective Conscious of Our American Juniors

Nearly every education major in colleges across the nation will run into a quote before they become teachers. The famous UCLA Basketball Coach John Wooden repeated it in a number of his speeches: "No written word, nor spoken plea can teach our youths what they should be, nor all the books in all the shelves, it's what the teachers are themselves."

To say that parents and coaches have significant influence over junior players both in the home and on the court would be stating the obvious. Coach Wooden, who, through the use of his Pyramid of Success among other things, guided his UCLA Basketball teams to a dynasty of ten National Championships that the sports world has to this day only seen since his time spent at the helm of that program. He embodied what he preached, and defined success as "peace of mind that is a direct result of self-satisfaction in knowing you made the effort to become the best that you are capable of becoming."

Winning, as you can see, is not addressed in this definition. And Coach Wooden was famous for never mentioning the word in his practices, and disallowed the usage of it among his players. Becoming the best player one could be at all times, being responsible for his own actions, giving the best effort both in training and in competition, and genuinely learning the craft were all qualities he demanded of his players, but more importantly it was qualities he embodied himself.

What is vital to our American tennis culture, among adults, parents, kids and coaches, is that this approach, this attitude becomes embraced on a mass scale. Rather than assuming talent is the main predictor of success, that mindsets are uncontrollable, that work ethic is innate, and that success is only up to the player – we as a culture can evolve toward having the resources and ability to create the environments that breed successful players. While nature is a factor, nurture is the predictor in the tennis world, which includes parenting, coaching, and training.

The Science of Success: Coach and Parent Roles

Anders Ericsson, Michael J. Prietula, and Edward T. Cokely, in an article entitled *The Making of An Expert* for the Harvard Business Review wrote, "Experts are always made, not born." They went on to say that the countless experts across a range of fields they examined had practiced intensively and deliberately, studied with devoted teachers and mentors, and had been supported enthusiastically by their families throughout their developing years.

The headline in their article reads "New research shows that outstanding performance is the product of years of deliberate practice and coaching, not of any innate talent or skill." When describing the deliberate practicing and coaching aspect of it, the authors wrote how mentors of experts taught them to coach themselves, encouraged and often forced their pupils to practice not only things they were good at, but also things "beyond their current level of competence and comfort."

Coaching, in an ideal sense, is a two-way street, where students receive messages, but also offer opinions and questions. More specifically, a good coach not only teaches their kids the fundamentals, but also shows their kids how to think for themselves, to problem-solve, and to understand the game and make their own decisions with awareness.

The same could be said for parenting. "Setting limits helps your child develop a sense of self-control. Encouraging independence helps her develop a sense of self-direction. To be successful in life, she's going to need both," wrote Laurence Steinberg, PHD, in his book *The Ten Basic Principles of Good Parenting.*

And of course everyone thinks they are a good tennis parent, just as every coach thinks they do a brilliant job. But to maximize one's capacity for striking a forehand, for example, certain elements of technique need to take place in the stroke – regardless of personal style and idiosyncrasy – as seen by the technical common denominators of the best pros on tour. And while being a smart player can mean different things for different people, pros also have, en masse, displayed a small range of shot selection choices in various situations that seem to work far better than others. As Ericsson puts it, "deliberate practice involves two kinds of learning: improving the skills you already have and extending the reach and range of your skills."

Either the coach has taught the most vital parameters of technique and tactics to the student or not, and students will inevitably become a reflection of their coaches ability or inability to think and communicate the nuances of the game clearly. What our American juniors and their parents need to constantly consider is whether or not this is happening during the time they have with their coaches – in addition to being more curious of said coaches track record and experience – partially as a player – and mostly as a coach. Players need not to judge themselves next to other players, but rather next to their own potential, and coaches are just as responsible for bringing out that potential as the players themselves.

Coaches must display an insatiable desire to absorb more information about how to teach the game if they expect their students to show a similar desire to constantly evolve as players. Parents must be the example within their own careers and occupations for their kids if they expect their offspring to develop a genuine need to see beyond limitations, to reach beyond the achievements of the average, and to plan every day toward becoming great at their craft.

It's all relative, as a good student does not always make a good teacher, just as a good player does not always make a good coach, unless said leader immerses him or herself into the profession and learns how to coach. While virtually everyone has been taught how to play the game, in the US it is rare to find a coach that has been taught by masters how to teach the game.

The qualities of successful people can be observed and measured, and identifying them can be helpful in creating the proverbial roadmap to raising a successful person and player.

Simple things like carrying your child's tennis bag, filling their water jug for them, making calls on their behalf to set up practices or lessons, signing them up for tournaments, talking to them or picking up the balls during their lessons, and waiting on their beckon call in a variety of ways can actually be harmful to the child's growth, particularly to the qualities of self-reliance, responsibility, and independence. Done as a favor once in a while is one thing, but…

While they are all acts of love, the child, when served like this, has virtually no responsibility for his own tennis career, and often develops a sense of entitlement. Players begin to expect things to be done for them, and develop little ability to do things on their own. Allowing, for example, kids to skip the pre-match jump rope and warm up routine to play video games on their iPods is hardly a way foster a focused mindset and a well-prepared strategy before walking out on court.

Deliberate Practice

Malcom Gladwell, in his bestselling book *Outliers*, made an effort similar to Ericsson and company in defining what it takes to become successful. Gladwell cites a range of studies that show that talent alone, or ability based on genetics, is a poor predictor of success. Culture, environment, personality, work ethic, parental support systems, and mentoring are far more accurate factors that predict ultimate success.

Specifically, he discusses the 10,000 Hour Rule, which says that it takes 10,000 hours of deliberate practice to become great at something. He cites Mozart (who was also cited by Ericsson and friends in the Harvard Business Review article), the Beatles, Michael Phelps, and many others that all spent over 10 years honing their skills under skilled mentors and practicing before producing truly great results.

Gladwell also discusses how greatness seems to require a certain minimum baseline amount of talent, which he calls "entrance criteria", but after that, the rest is explainable by the following factors.

Cultural and economic issues aside, many of the most successful tennis players have similar characteristics and upbringing. They all have had at least 10,000 hours of deliberate practice, most or all of which with good coaching.

And most of them had the following elements either available or instilled in them growing up: Mentoring and good on court coaching, personality and work ethic, parental guidance and support, self-reliance, confidence and belief, consistent goal setting: short term and long term, and a competition and practice pathway that promotes both playing under pressure and exposure to new and different levels of play.

What the 10,000 Hour Rule exemplifies is a "How To" guide of *immersion*. Dictionary.com defines immersion as "a state of being deeply engaged or involved; absorption." Having 10,000 hours of deliberate practice can mean different things to different people, but essentially it comes down to a simple idea: you will get out of your tennis career what you put into it. By creating the environment that contains the checklist of aspects listed above, you can create a roadmap for yourself that can help you further immerse yourself in the game.

What Gladwell does not say - and any good coach would concur - is that 10,000 hours of practice will make you great at something. What he does say is that 10,000 hours of *deliberate* practice can make you great at something. For us in the tennis world, that means surrounding yourself with the right people, the right coaches, having a plan for each practice, and constantly looking to develop your own character on the court, your own tactical and strategic abilities, and certainly your own technique for each stroke.

The idea that knowledge is power is what Gladwell implies in his description of deliberate practice. Practice alone on the court for hours and hours will only take you so far. Greatness, however, is spawned from playing and practicing with the intention of learning more about how exactly you wish to hit the ball, where you want to hit in a range of point scenarios, and why. And there are plenty of examples of this, like knowing where your elbow should be when you make contact, the positioning of your wrist during your backswing, defining when to use an open stance, what it means to play good defense, how exactly to brush across the ball on a kick serve, how to generate positive energy in between points, and so on.

These are just a few examples of short-term assignments that can be focused on each day or each week - that exemplify deliberate practice. Greatness comes from focusing on small tasks every day that build toward a larger goal. A good practice is not one where a student hits a million balls, but rather one where the student walks away from the experience of practicing and *knows more* about how he wants to do things.

A truly immersed player discusses with his coach regularly how to swell his strengths, identify and find solutions for his weaknesses, and constantly looks to evolve as a player, as a person, and looks to get better every day. The capacity for self-reliance and knowledge of how their strokes work and why is one major contributing component to confidence on court.

The pride produced by daily reinforcement of process-oriented thinking versus result-oriented thinking can easily be seen through the body language of players particularly in between points during matches. Players that are obsessed more with their level of play and the details that cause the ebbs and flows of their own execution – instead of the end result – are the players that ultimately find more joy in the sport and as a consequence more success.

Talent and Success: "Greatness isn't born, it's grown"

Greatness seems to require a certain amount of ability, or "entrance criteria", as Gladwell and others have mentioned, but studies have shown that talent - however defined - is a poor predictor. Of course, a certain baseline amount of talent is required of all great athletes, but the Geoff Colvin book entitled *Talent is Overrated* discusses why culture, environment, work ethic, personality, and mentorship are all far better predictors of success than talent in a similar way that *Outliers* tackles the issue. Daniel Coyle's book *The Talent Code* gives a "How To" for its headline "Greatness isn't born, it's grown," and the list of these recent studies goes on and on.

Becoming a great player does require some talent – which perhaps could mean physical agility and the intellectual capacity to understand how and why hitting the ball can work. The idea here though is that once you reach a certain point, talent will only take you so far. For example, experienced players and coaches have witnessed a number of players with all the physical gifts that a player could ever want – and beautiful strokes as well – and that same person could rarely win a match that really mattered.

A top nationally ranked player would consider someone like this common, and certainly one who never was able to become a smart player that possessed genuine toughness and resolve for whatever reason.

What nearly all success stories, particularly in the game of tennis, have in common – is that they have found a way to create an environment for themselves that contains the list of factors mentioned in this article. Ambition, resources, guidance, and wisdom are the characteristics that most often separate the most successful players from everyone else.

Jeff Greenwald, a former touring pro, current author, and sports psychologist in northern California, agreed with these ideas on USTA Player Development Talk Radio (that I hosted for a brief time). He said on the show that these characteristics, when they all exist genuinely within one athlete, result in a person that sustains a good work ethic over a long period of time. These athletes end of having the discipline to work hard each week and each month, where they develop the skills they already have and add more skills to their arsenal all the time.

In that same radio show, ATP Tour Coach and former Russian Davis Cup Coach Vitaly Gorin added that, "It's easy for kids – and even parents – to commit to really working hard for a month or two. They come out to the courts twice a day and give it everything they've got and it's great. But having the discipline to work hard consistently over time is really what defines someone's career. If I had to say what the most important quality is that I look for in a player – it's not technique and it's not talent, though it used to be when I was a younger coach. Now, after having seen so many talented players fall short of their potential, and so many marginally gifted players make it much farther than anyone dreamed of, I would say the biggest thing I look for in a player is commitment."

To Vitaly's point – and Mr. Greenwald's as well, the committed players find the resources, they find the coaching and mentors, and their commitment breeds ambition.

Process versus Result Oriented Thinking

"You can outscore people and lose at times, and you can be outscored on court and still be a winner at times, and I feel that doing all the things that allow you to give your best effort makes you successful in my book," said Coach Wooden.

Jerry Lynch, former National Championship winning Men's Tennis Coach at University of California at Santa Cruz, takes Wooden's sentiments a step further. "We are a society obsessed with winning. When stressed about the outcomes, your body is unable to move with the fluidity or flow that so necessary for a winning performance. Your greatest triumphs are always the byproducts of your ability to demonstrate the level you have attained in anything you do… You do this by focusing on the moment, the experience itself, rather than by trying to control the outcome or results… With such awareness, you are in position for sustained success in athletics and in life."

To say that that this attitude is widespread among athletes today in the tennis world would be a gross exaggeration. To say even that this attitude permeates the draws of the most elite tournaments in the continental US would be equally drastic, but establishing such a collective conscious of our American juniors is certainly a possibility.

As the game has evolved with new equipment – new racquet and string technology – it fostered refined techniques for hitting every shot imaginable, enhanced fitness directives, and so on. The game can also evolve in the realm of emotional fitness, psychological strength, a better definition of success, and an exponentially increased priority on development instead of results. If a player has a wide array of tools to use on the court, he or she must know how to use them, understand how to focus on using them, and not be afraid to use them.

Because players today often have the ability to hit more types of shots with technical proficiency, there is a need for process-oriented thinking now more than ever within the sport. With more tools in their possession, players now have more they can focus on. Instead of obsessing with winning and losing and outcomes, players should focus on how to use the tools they have in the next point, the next game, and the next set.

Players that show frustration after losing a point in a match because they didn't win it are wasting their energy and are exercising their outcome-oriented thought process. Their body language droops and their frustration is written all over their faces. A process-oriented thinker is far too busy to worry about results of winning points or games or matches, because the process-oriented thinker has habits that involve the focus of performing at the highest level possible.

They have no time for moping around because of their in between points routine composed of three parts. This routine is composed of brief, instantaneous responses to 1) why they made or missed a shot, 2) why their shot selection in the last point worked or didn't, and 3) as they walk up to the line to prepare to serve or return, they have some idea of how they wish to ideally play the next point.

By practicing these three steps in the between point routine, players can have an awareness of how their thoughts contribute to their performance, how much they can focus on finding solutions to performance by simply investing one or two seconds in between points into it, and discover how their thoughts control their body language and ability to concentrate on the present moment.

*   *   *   *

Parents, often without realizing it, always contribute to this – one way or another. By showing frustration when a child misses a shot or loses a match, by constantly looking online to discover ranking information, by displaying disappointment over results instead of considering the overall performance, parents contribute to a result-oriented thinking player. This player is so distracted by winning and the fear of losing (or fear of disappointing mom or dad) that he or she cannot fully be in the present moment and focus on executing technique and making sound decisions on court with purpose and on purpose.

Placing labels on kids inside the home can contribute to outcome oriented thinking as well, even when they are well intentioned. When a mother tells her son that he is so smart when he gets a math problem wrong, she is not rewarding the work he put in to get the problem right. She is telling him that he got it correct because of something he is naturally, which ingrains in the child a certain sense himself not being responsible for his own abilities – which they are not fully in his control. Were the mother to tell her son that she was proud of him for putting in the effort to understand the material and find the right answer, the boy would have a sense of work ethic ingrained in him – that all things are possible with the right amount of commitment and work ethic. He would then begin to take ownership over his work ethic over time, with constant reinforcement from his mother in this respect, when it comes to his math homework, and probably everything else he does.

Labels of a more negative nature can be even more harmful. When a father says to his daughter "You are so lazy", the effects are the same described above, except more pronounced and emotional for the kid. Asking the daughter not to be lazy right now avoids the label, but encouraging her to be more productive in the moment could be a method of getting the message across, avoiding a label, and producing a more positive environment. Keeping comments in context within a moment-to-moment situation as a parent will instinctively influence the child to do the same. It also helps avoid identity crises in the kids as they grow up, since the labels – whatever they are – can stick to the kids like glue. Without labels in their lives, and with a parental influence of work ethic and process-oriented thinking will be the utmost factors in their success, kids will begin to believe in themselves more and more and become independent thinkers and doers.

The parallels of these concepts in regards a child's tennis – or a person's tennis for that matter – are not difficult to imagine. Labels of being a cheater, or a choke artist, a loser, or whatever can cause damage to the psyche of a player – in a potentially permanent way. Labels create the opposite of the growth mindset, which is the fixed mindset, where kids and people see themselves as being capable of only so much, and that's that. Labels cause a mindset that one has been dealt a proverbial set of cards about their own abilities and personality, and that their character and talents are trapped inside the box that the labels create.

Players who believe themselves only capable of so much because of such labels tend to limit themselves in a range of ways. Often such labels can negatively influence a player's work ethic because they believe working hard to be futile, given their own set of labeled circumstances. Players who have been called a "winner" or something to that effect, with that label placed upon them consistently, may also be prone to not putting in the work necessary to perform at their peak, because they may feel that they are winners regardless of their work ethic and that winning is just a god-given ability they have. This attitude hardly fosters peak performance, nor does it foster evolution or ambition.

On the other hand, players who believe they can accomplish whatever they want – if they put in the time, the effort, the thought, and the dedication – are usually right. And this attitude often comes from parental guidance and influence.

Process-oriented thinkers typically have little to no issues with combating fear, since the fear does not usually exist for them while competing. Players who focus on doing all the things necessary that give them the best chance to perform at their peak rarely have problems with choking, with getting nervous before or during matches, or with anxiety-caused injuries. This is because they are so focused on implementing technique and footwork and decision-making on court, or scouting opponents and developing pre-match strategies, that they often do not have time for worrying about winning and losing.

They understand that winning and losing are by-products of doing the things the right way or not, and that by paying attention to the details – driven by performance-based thinking – they give themselves the opportunity to compete at the highest levels they are capable each day. Process-oriented thinkers typically have parents and coaches that convey a consistent message that winning a tennis match does make one a winning person, and that losing a tennis match does not make one a loser. They instead have leaders in their lives that encourage a sense of urgency in maximizing each moment of training and competition for the sake of self-growth and enjoyment.

An ideal parent is supportive of good behavior, good effort, and makes NO effort to coach the child on their forehand and backhand. As pattern detectors, kids see the desire parents have to win and therefore internalize pressure on themselves as a result. On the flip side, kids also see parents being primarily interested in good behavior, good effort and focus, and using each experience on court to grow as a person and as a player. Either way, kids will behave accordingly so as to please the parent.

It would be ridiculous to think that a carpenter would be able to do the job of an astronomer, just as it would be ridiculous to expect an accountant to do the work of an architect. An ideal world has the coaches coaching and the parents parenting. Parents, in this ideal world, offer consistent, unconditional love and support, without criticizing technique or shot selection.

What it Takes

The following was taken from the AP news posting in August of 2010, and highlights a quote from WTA touring pro Maria Kirilienko, who has had relative quality resources and coaching throughout her career:

In an all-Russian quarterfinal, Maria Kirilenko beat Dinara Safina 6-3, 6-3. Kirilenko said she's not surprised so many Russians are doing so well on the Tour. "We work a lot," she said. "That's why I think we have good results, you know. Because to have a talent, it's not enough. You have to be patient. You have to work a lot. You have to fight. Everything together. So I think that's why we have so many Russians."

Thomas Edison once said, "Being busy does not always mean real work. The object of all work is production or accomplishment and to either of these ends there must be forethought, system, planning, intelligence, and honest purpose, as well as perspiration. Seeming to do is not doing."

It is this commitment and attitude that our American juniors can easily possess. By focusing on the development instead of rankings, and the constant concentration on becoming the best player possible rather than the so-called need to win certain tournaments or achieve certain rankings, we as a nation can begin to produce a much larger pool of players that are reaching their potential and enjoying the journey of their playing careers. It is this commitment, however, that will remain forever out of reach for our American juniors that grow into adults without a clear message coming from within the home and from their mentors and coaches.

Coaches must educate players and parents about what it means to work hard – and how they can work smart each week. This means having a fitness regimen, having regularly scheduled private lessons with a master coach and multiple opportunities each week for players to compete against their peers. This means possessing a growth mindset (more on that later) and always looking to get better, and this also means parents that push their kids (only) when the need to be pushed.

As Sam Ewing once said, "Hard work spotlights the character of people: some turn up their sleeves, some turn up their noses, and some don't turn up at all."

*   *   *   *

This is a game that exposes who a person is, how they react or respond to adversity, how they handle success and work towards it, how patient they are, how good they are to themselves, how patient they are, how understanding of others, how vengeful they can be, how temperamental, how ambitious, and what kind of sense of self they have. The good thing about tennis is that there is no place to hide on the court, no one to pass the ball to, no possible way to avoid facing the competition, and no way to avoid facing yourself. There truly is no place to hide.

You can't hit three home runs and see your team lose, and you can't miss all your free throws and play poor defense and still see your team win. You can't roll the dice and get lucky, and you can't hope your teammate scores a goal.

It's only you out there on court, and either you are happy with yourself, confident in your own game, you believe in the work you have put in, and you have faith in your ability to perform well moment to moment, or you don't. Either you are scared of success, or achieving your personal best, or you are not. Either you look across the net at your opponent in fear, or you don't. Either you have put the necessary work and thought and commitment into your game to allow for your personal best come out in the prior weeks and months, or you haven't. And either you think about the process, or you obsess with the result.

Tennis is a very honest sport. Players that are honest with themselves on court have the edge.

Parenting Do's	Parenting Don'ts
- Hold emotionally intelligent discussions about tennis - Provide love and support regardless of match outcomes - Act calm and confident during matches - Provide ample opportunity and resources for your child to be successful - Make your child responsible for tennis preparation – equipment ready, calling partner to hit with, etc. - Have a stable home life - Emphasize player development, fun, and learning over winning and rankings - Keep success in perspective - Expose your child to a few different sports and activities - Hold your child accountable for poor behaviors on court - Push your child to practice when lazy - Encourage your child to seek out opportunities and challenges - Model an active lifestyle and healthy eating habits - Emphasize core values, such as, "if you are going to do it, do it right" - Emphasize the importance of hard work, and how work ethic is a better predictor of success than talent - Provide transportation, financial, and logistical support - Recognize and encourage your child when he/she does something right - Help make tennis fun	- Focus the majority of conversations at home about tennis - Criticize your child about his/her tennis - Critique your child immediately after the match or during the car ride home - Exert pressure on them to win - Treat your child differently dependent on whether he/she won or lost - Focus on short term winning/results instead of long term development - Put your interests ahead of your child's in tennis - Consider your child's tennis as an investment for which you should receive something in return - Never allow your child some "say" in tennis decisions - Coaching your child when it is hurting parent-child relationships - Telling your child that his/her opponent is not good and he/she should beat them easily - Consider your child a tennis player first, and a son or daughter second - Show no interest in your child's tennis - Obsess over rankings - Encourage gamesmanship or cheating to achieve a result - Correct your child's technique or strategy during practice matches in a frustrated manner - Change coaches constantly

Success Formula: coaching + training + resources + positive parenting + process-oriented thinking + independence + commitment + ambition = *reaching one's potential.*

Chapter 2.

Learning A Game Taught Upside Down

In February 1878, the first telephone book was published in New Haven, Connecticut. The book was one page long and had fifty names in it.

In a similar vein, the game of tennis has advanced about as much as our phone books have grown in size. With racquet and string technology providing greater opportunities to strike the ball with more spin and power, and newer generations learning from the strengths and weaknesses of their predecessors, the game is played at a higher level now than ever. Examining the sophistication of the techniques and tactical prowess of a top 20 ATP Tour player today is quite a different study than analyzing one from the 1970's.

Players today possess a wide range of tools to hurt their opponents with, and to keep up with the competition, players must become as complete as possible and be able to hit every shot in the book.

Tennis is a game that essentially is taught upside down, which is a phrase Jose Higueras said to me numerous times. What that means, simply put, is that the most important aspect of the game is how a player uses his mind, and how a player recognizes opportunities and decides to respond to various situations. The second most important aspect would be footwork, of course, and how a player moves to the ball, his or her fitness, and the way a player gets in position for each shot with the feet. The third most vital part of a player's game would be the hands and body, in other words – how the player hits the ball and what type of technique he or she uses.

But a good coach will teach these to a student in the opposite order. A good coach will teach the hands and unit turn first. How to set the wrist and make a loop on a ground stroke, for example, where the contact point is, how to brush up or slice and follow through, and so on. Once a player understands how to hit a good ball, and has a solid grasp of the fundamentals with the hands and unit turn, then the coach will teach the student how to use these fundamentals in motion – on the move. The ability to move to the ball with good footwork and then hit with solid fundamentals with the hands and unit turn is the second skill learned in this progression.

Once a player can hit a good ball on the move, then a good coach will begin teaching the student tactics and strategy. There's no reason to teach a kid shot selection and decision-making if they can't hit the ball very well in the first place.

It's really a walk before you run progression of coaching. Once the technique is in place, now the coach can begin molding the student's ability to make decisions based on various offensive, defensive, and neutral positions on the court.

*   *   *   *

Three Areas

"All things are difficult before they are easy," Thomas Fuller once said.

So the question that must be – hopefully – on your mind, is, are these things all possible to teach at once? Can't you build these fundamentals together? You would be an ambitious parent or coach if you were asking. And, to be honest, I like your zeal.

Well, sort of. Each of the concepts can be introduced – and *progressively* they can be incorporated over time. Think of tennis as a recipe with three equal parts.

Visualize three parts: 1 that represents technique with the hands and body, another that represents feet, and the third area representing the eyes and mind.

Teaching the Hands and Unit Turn First – Mostly...

So imagine you are teaching a beginner, or raising a beginner. As they are learning how to set their wrist and begin their loop on their forehand, where to make contact, how to brush up to hit topspin, and how to follow through, they should also be learning how to rotate or turn the hips and shoulders. They should be learning to rotate their shoulders close to 180 degrees from start to finish, and they should be learning how to brush up the back of the ball with a set wrist before they accelerate on the follow through over their shoulder.

And as that process evolves, they can also learn to hit with margin for error and net clearance and consistency – and even accelerate through short balls. And as they learn to hit a good ball – with good technique – a coach can promote ever so slightly over time to hit harder on easier shots and higher and softer on more difficult shots so as to introduce the notions of offense and defense that they will later master.

Teaching the Feet Second – Mostly...

Little by little, the player, with his newfound technique, can begin to master how to move his or her feet and use these strokes in motion, how to set the feet or get in position with the legs for each shot. They can learn to split step and move to the ball while turned, and how to make an open stance or a closed/square stance for forehands and backhands.

Teaching the Eyes and Mind Third – Mostly...

And finally of course, learning how to play a point, how to set up a point and create short balls to attack, leaning various positions in the court and proper responses with shot selection all can become a process of growth at this time.

So the stages of learning are really a 3 part series, none of which are entirely mutually exclusive. And as technique is taught, the best drills also develop instincts of tactical shot selection. The stages of learning are best taught and executed with overlap to maximize the acceleration of the player's growth. In other words, the kids can be taught directly one thing while placed in an environment or exercise that naturally develops the instincts of something else.

The Psychology of Learning the Fundamentals

There is research to back up the validity of these concepts of learning in ordered, staged progressions that grow more complex over time. Learning expert Donald Clark wrote in his blog entitled *Plan B: 10 Facts about learning...* that spaced learning, or practicing in spaced out intervals with concentrated attention on a only a few things is where the most effective learning takes place, regardless of the subject matter.

"We forget things quickly and that the most effective way to prevent this forgetting is to practice at spaced intervals over time. Knowledge is easy to learn but hard to retain," he said. He goes on to comment that too much information at one time can contribute to what he calls "cognitive overload", that the order of which things are learned is critical to how knowledge is stored in the brain, and that people are more inclined to learn from visual stimuli than text they read or words they hear. In other words, throwing a wide range of information into a beginning student's brain can not just cause information overload and stunt the learning process, but also the order at which things are learned have a great deal how student's will be able to move forward with and implement the concepts they've been exposed to. So showing the kids what to do – and the order at which they show it and teach it – has as much impact if not more on how they develop as what one tells them what to do.

The field of psychology has decades of research regarding the methods of learning, but essentially the research shows that when skilled mentors introduce progressively more complex information to cognitively active – or engaged students – in an environment that promotes and demands deliberate practice – tangible, effective learning occurs. Deliberate practice, as has been previously mentioned, takes place when mentors incur imposed knowledge upon students that question the teacher and the methods, where the communication is a two-way street, and where the student is encouraged to develop the skills they have already as well as the skills they could possess.

Behaviorists say that learning can be analyzed on changes in behavior – and for our purposes the evolution of fundamentals in stroke and tactical production – and that environment shapes one's behavior; what one learns is determined by the elements in the environment. They also say that the principles of contiguity (how close in time two events must be for a bond to be formed) and reinforcement (any means of increasing the likelihood that an event will be repeated) are central to explaining the learning process. So, for a player, the coaching, the parental influences in the home, and peer influence would be examples of models that the student would learn from and consequently model.

This idea is closely connected to the social learning theory, where observational learning takes place in social settings. Educators work so that learners are part of a community process so they can understand how different people behave, develop relationships, and learn from the experiences taking place within those relationships.

Where behaviorists looked to the environment, those drawing on Gestalt turned to the individual's mental processes. In other words, they were concerned with cognition - the act or process of knowing. Researchers like Jean Piaget, while recognizing the contribution of environment, explored changes in internal cognitive structure. He identified four stages of mental growth (sensorimotor, preoperational, concrete operational and formal operational). Jerome Bruner explored how mental processes could be linked to teaching – emphasizing, among other things, learning through discovery. Robert M. Gagné developed a model that highlighted eight different forms of learning – where he pointed out that behaviorists identified only a fragment of human capabilities.

With that said, let's explore what the practical parts for our needs are that cognitive psychologists found. In 1998 James Hartley drew out some of the key principles of learning associated with cognitive psychology. He said, "Learning results from inferences, expectations and making connections. Instead of acquiring habits, learners acquire plans and strategies, and prior knowledge is important."

The principles Hartley identified were: 1) Instruction should be well organized. Well-organized materials are easier to learn and to remember. 2) Instruction should be clearly structured. Subject matters are said to have inherent structures - logical relationships between key ideas and concepts – that link the parts together.

3) Prior knowledge is important. Things must fit with what is already known if it is to be learnt. 4) Differences between individuals are important, as they will affect learning. Differences in 'cognitive style' or methods of approach influence learning. 5) Cognitive feedback gives information to learners about their success or failure concerning the task at hand. Reinforcement can come through giving information - a 'knowledge of results' - rather than simply a reward.

So in the game of tennis, taking lessons from 3 to 5 different coaches in the early stages of a players development can not just cause information overload, but also these different coaches may present information in varying structures and organization as well as with different expectations and reinforcements. So it is important for a young player to have some consistency with who they work with and what direction they are going with their tennis, with their strokes, with their evolution as competitors, etc., so as to provide a stable environment for the player learn the game the right way.

Abraham Maslow's hierarchy of motivation touches heavily upon the humanistic orientation of learning. Once you get past the basic human instinctual desires for physical health and safety, the hierarchy he outlines then includes love and belongingness – which is the desire to create meaningful friendships, and self esteem – which involves the desire for strength, achievement, competence and mastery, and the development of confidence from establishing independence, reputation, and prestige. Finally, Maslow said that people seek out self-actualization – which is the full use and expression of talents, capacities and potentialities.

Self actualizers can submit to social regulation without losing their own integrity or personal independence, and often they may follow a social norm without their horizons being bounded in the sense that they fail to see or consider other possibilities. They are capable of transcending the socially prescribed ways of acting, and achieving this level may mean developing to the full stature of which they are capable.

As these basic human needs Maslow outlines lay deeply within all of us, what parents and coaches can do is look to highlight how a player can put these elements in place within their tennis careers, and move toward becoming a self-actualizer. If players are aware of these basic human needs deeply embedded within themselves, they can more clearly prioritize what is important to them in both the day to day and the big picture.

By have a basic understanding of hierarchy of needs – and a basic understanding of the qualities they should be striving for – players can more effectively build for themselves a proverbial roadmap to success. They can begin to take charge of their own tennis careers and realize the full use and expression of their talents and potential. This taking charge of the player's tennis career ultimately reaps benefits in a wide array of areas within the life of a tennis player – and the humanistic orientation to learning that Maslow outlined was expanded upon by a man named Carl Rogers, who discussed in his work how the learner can become more involved in the learning process.

Rogers' passion for education was evident in his work, which engaged the whole person and their experiences. His message that learning combines the logical and intuitive as well as the intellect and feelings was broken into a few parts. To put it another way, as Clay P. Bedford once said, "You can teach a student a lesson for a day; but if you can teach him to learn by creating curiosity, he will continue the learning process as long as he lives."

Rogers saw the following elements as being involved in significant or experiential learning. 1) It has a quality of personal involvement – the whole person in both feeling and cognitive aspects being in the learning event. 2) It is self-initiated. Even when the impetus or stimulus comes from the outside, the sense of discovers of reaching out, of grasping and comprehending, comes from within. 3) It is pervasive. It makes a difference in the behavior, the attitudes, perhaps even the personality of the learner. 4) It is evaluated by the learner. She knows whether it is meeting her need, whether it leads toward what she wants to know, whether it illuminates the dark area of ignorance she is experiencing. The locus of evaluation resides definitely in the learner. 5) Its essence is meaning. When such learning takes place, the element of meaning to the learner is built into the whole experience.

In addition to behaviorist's learning theory, the cognitive, and the humanistic learning theories, social learning theory – as mentioned briefly above – seems to play an important role not just in child development but in general human development. Certainly one can imagine observing others and learning from their behavior, and in this sense – putting players in group settings or where they can play and compete with their peers is major aspect of the learning process. Players don't just learn by listening and doing, they also learn by observing their peers and watching how they do things, especially when there is a social element to it.

As a player develops his or her game, the presence of peers who are also developing their games at a similar level is important because not only provides motivation to compete successfully against the people they see regularly, but also it makes playing fun because he or she is doing so with friends. Social relationships play a significant role in supporting a player and determining how long he or she participates in the sport, especially early in their careers – since peers give new students another good reason to show up to the courts and thus enhances commitment to the game.

Seeing the Big Picture

As these stages of learning – the three buckets of hands/unit turn, footwork, and the eyes and mind – are being taught, what makes the stages most effective is relating the material to the student's life, encouraging the student's own sense of involvement in the process of learning (the aforementioned two-way street of communication between player and coach), how the life skills learned on court permeate into the lifestyle of the player off the court, and the meaning that the student assigns to the material covered and learned skills on court. So that act of coaches and parents not just providing a structured environment where learning and development is inevitable, but also the act of asking questions that lead the students to discovery of principles that promote the fundamentals and work ethic can be one example of the practical application of the execution of raising a champion.

The subsequent changes of behavior and evolution of personal life skills developed in the player – displayed both on and off the court – become a gauge for the effectiveness of the training a player is getting throughout the course of his or her development. And obviously the changes over time in stroke production and the acquisition and perfection of the technical and tactical fundaments are also a gauge.

Such evolution can be predicted by the level of commitment by the player to the game and his or her progress, the types of goals they are setting for themselves, and so on. However, it is common for young students to be very impressionable during the early stages of their tennis careers, and they are more likely to develop commitment to the game when they are challenged to develop life skills outlined above in addition to learning how to hit topspin or follow through on a forehand.

If coaches and parents alike show kids and new students to the game how tennis can develop the self, and if they can simultaneously create an avid curiosity within the young player, the students will be more likely to gain an increased interest in the sport early on and thus more players will become committed to the game. Providing a structured learning environment will also only make the game easier to learn, and players that see success right off the bat, so to speak, in tennis, will be more likely to want to continue playing. Such an environment that also provides significant social opportunities for players offers chances to make friends, create relationships, and thus more learning opportunities through observation and modeling.

Having a step-by-step progression of how to teach tennis – which is appropriately overlapped – will help create an environment on the court that gives relative rookies to the game a vision of how they can become a good player over the course of a short period of time. Giving the kids a structured environment where they can first process consistent themes about the hands and unit turn first over time with slow introductions of footwork, and then consistent themes of footwork within the context of fine tuning the hands and unit turn techniques as well as introducing basic tactical concepts, and finally the orientation of tactics and strategy while performing maintenance on the fundamentals previously learned, students will have a clear roadmap in the short and long run of their development.

When the messages in this model are regularly administered and reliable, and growing in complexity over time as the player shows he or she is ready to move forward in the process, maximum acceleration of growth is not just possible but also probable.

Taking Ownership

In the words of Clay P. Bedford, "You can teach a student a lesson for a day; but if you can teach him to learn by creating curiosity, he will continue the learning process as long as he lives."

The human brain has about 100 billion neurons. If the average human brain were a computer, the storage capacity would exceed four terabytes. So the way we think needs some structure, and leadership in a player's life can be a major source of providing organization of how a player thinks, sees himself, focuses on various tasks, and understands how the game of tennis fits into their lives.

With coaches and parents that promote to their kids an understanding their basic human needs and how to look for and find ways of satisfying them – the students will also see with foreknowledge the skills they will learn on the court and how such skills can improve their lives. As the previous chapter focused in part of the science of success and achievement, the movement that new students have toward developing specific personal qualities – which Maslow and Rogers highlight – through the teaching methods that the behaviorist psychologists point out – can be swift and smooth.

More importantly, the students can take ownership of their own learning process. With foreknowledge of the benefits they receive through the growth process of competing, and an understanding of what the goals are and how they can achieve them, they can be in charge of their own development and activate their own motives for training and learning. Students without a direction or roadmap of where they were in their development, where they are, and where they are going to be with training and a specific series of tasks to be learned, often lack motivation and ambition. Student that have the guidance of mentors and coaches who can direct the student toward setting goals and providing the learning environment that enables both short term and long term goals to be within reach, students often find that the drive to work hard comes naturally to them.

If the student is taught the skills to properly prepare for each practice, for each match in a tournament, and for each fitness routine, they will likely – with the right goals, the right roadmap, and the right leadership in their lives – have the motivation to take ownership of many parts of their tennis. They will be more likely, if educated, to warm up properly before matches, to jump rope and stretch before practices, to visualize peak performance with positive imagery, and to check their arousal and energy levels before stepping onto the court – and adjust accordingly if needed.

Coaches can encourage and teach their students to use visualization – to see themselves hitting the right shots in the right way, to see themselves with guided imagery building their own confidence through positive self talk – during pre-match or pre-practice preparation to facilitate full engagement and concentration. With mental rehearsal, minds and bodies become trained to actually perform the skill imagined.

Coaches also can educate students about arousal and energy levels before stepping onto the court and during play to increase optimum performance. While different people perform their best at different levels of arousal and energy levels, according to the psychological arousal theory entitled *Individual Zones of Optimal Functioning Theory,* coaches can work with the students to find what works for them. There are more than 640 muscles in the human body – and all of them need to be poised and ready to perform before and during each match and practice. Too much energy can lead to anxiety, tighten muscles, and affect coordination – which is what we call "choking", but not enough energy leads to flat, uninspired performances.

The Anxiety Direction and Intensity Theory states that how someone sees their own anxiety is important for understanding the relationship of their anxiety to their performance. Both the person's interpretation of the intensity (how much anxiety) and the direction (whether the anxiety is helping or hindering their performance) have to be considered. Therefore, viewing anxiety as helpful leads to better performance.

The more ownership a student takes over preparation for practices and matches, the more ownership the player likely takes over all other aspects of his or her tennis career. Managing one's arousal and energy can influence and increase a player's ability to take ownership. Mentally rehearsing ideal performance can also further activate a player's motivation and desire to continue developing with a sense of urgency. Students that take ownership over their learning processes and development more often display poise and the right amount of energy during practices and tournaments because they are fully engaged in what they are doing.

*   *   *   *

Chapter 3.

Coaching Philosophy

Webster defines leadership with one word: influence. As John C. Maxwell put it, "A leader is one who knows the way, goes the way, and shows the way."
In addition to being to teach the nuances of technique, offense and defense, point construction, footwork, and strategy, *Leading with Vision: The Bridge Builder* is a poem that describes the vision a coach must have.

> An old man, going a lone highway,
> Came, at the evening, cold and gray,
> To a chasm, vast, and deep, and wide,
> Through which was flowing a sullen tide.
> The old man crossed in the twilight dim;
> The sullen stream had no fear for him;
> But he turned, when safe on the other side,
> And built a bridge to span the tide.
> "Old man," said a fellow pilgrim, near,
> "You are wasting strength with building here;
> Your journey will end with the ending day;
> You never again will pass this way;
> You've crossed the chasm, deep and wide-
> Why build you this bridge at the evening tide?"
> The builder lifted his old gray head:
> "Good friend, in the path I have come," he said,
> "There followeth after me today,
> A youth, whose feet must pass this way.
> This chasm, that has been naught to me,
> To that fair-haired youth may a pitfall be.
> He, too, must cross in the twilight dim;
> *Good friend, I am building this bridge for him."*
> - Will Allen Dromgoole

Having a coaching philosophy is important on every level of coaching, and it's a big part of being a leader. It clarifies the coach's mind on essential aspects of his building a champion. It also helps clarify the developmental planning for the athletes and their parents – and lets them know what the goals are for everyone involved. By having this information available from the beginning, it helps prevent future problems and keeps the coach and the student on a clearly defined path.
A lot of coaches may have good answers to problems within a student's game. But without the ability to communicate effectively the necessary messages to the player as well as generate a genuine interest within the student to develop the skills in question, having good answers does not do a lot of good for anyone. However, if a coach – without a personal ego in the way – genuinely seeks to help the student for

the sake of the student – not the coach, then the player will respond.

Coaches that operate on court with the intention of throwing information at their students and expecting them to just do what they say for their own good miss out on a fundamental principle of teaching. The notion of "arousing an eager want" in a student can do more good than any amount of pushing information towards a player. In other words, inspiring a player to develop a real desire to evolve not just in a particular way but overall will, over time, be a far more effective coaching style. Inspiring players to want to get better in certain areas by explaining the benefits and rewards of improving this or that area of their game yields infinitely more powerful and lasting results.

If a player knows why refining and re-defining their forehand footwork, for example, how it will enable them to be in better position for the ball, make the execution of the shot easier, give them the ability to take the ball earlier and facilitate a quicker recovery, and so on, the player will be dramatically more likely to put in the work to make the change. On the other side of the coin, when a coach just orders the player to hit an open stance in this situation or that, with no explanation of why it will help the player, no change is probable.

Players, however old or mature, intuitively can sense when coaches are telling them to do something instead of encouraging them, and students can also sense when the coach is demanding things for the sake exercising his or her own ego instead offering a no strings attached, benevolent piece of advice. Said John Wooden, "Make sure that team members know that they are working with you, not for you."

A clear philosophy will gives a coach and student a foundation upon which to work together to base decisions. Coaches don't always give much consideration to what they are trying to accomplish. Without clearly defined goals and incentives, a result-oriented climate can likely ensue. If, typically, a coach is only concerned with wins and losses, he will wind up with unhappy students and dissatisfaction with the program, with lessons, with practice regimens, and tournament performance. Ultimately, being a coach can mean a lot of things. But the not so subtle implication here in this book is that in the best of circumstances, it means the promotion of skill acquisition, the development of a growth mindset, creating an environment where fundamentals are obvious and deliberately discussed, and the outlining of how the game can and will expand life skills of the student.

We've covered the basis of teaching skill acquisition with the bucket list, and with the outline of how to use this progressive method of teaching strokes, tactics and footwork. The following chapters will first introduce core concepts of technique and footwork and then expand upon tactical and strategic concepts. One is not a complete coach if he or she cannot teach beginners solid fundamentals or guide pros to expanding their skill sets and making good decisions on court – and being able to do only one or the other well, while admirable – still makes for an incomplete coach.

Coaches that possess a tangible philosophy about constant evolution and growth are likely to be learners themselves – and are likely to be coaches who get better at coaching each week, just as their students probably do.

But regardless of the type of student one has, teaching a growth mindset can transform both the student and coach. Stanford Psychologist Carol Dweck, as mentioned in a previous chapter, wrote about this in her book in explaining the mindset for achievement. Creating curiosity in people is a significant theme in her book, which cites a range of studies that show results of kids focused on outcome with average to poor performance and kids focused on learning and the process of doing with well above average to excellent performance in all kinds of different scenarios.

Dweck quotes Benjamin Barber, an eminent sociologist, who once said, "I don't divide the world into the weak and the strong, or the successes and the failures... I divide the world into the learners and non-learners." Her book discusses how to promote the growth mindset to parents and coaches and business leaders and more, which is the instilled message to others that "you are a developing person and I am interested in your development." That message is diametrically opposed to what kids and employees and students hear often from their parents or coaches or business leaders, which is "you have permanent traits and I'm judging them." So the notion that we are all constantly evolving does a great deal of good for all involved – both the giver and receiver of this message, since it ingrains the philosophy both from within the speaker and the listener.

Having a Mentor, Defining a Mentor

Underlying all of this of course is the idea that, while today there are many different tennis programs that one can join and different people to play with and listen to, having a consistent mentor can open so many doors of growth for a player, since with a consistent mentor is a student's life, all of these things we are discussing become possible. There are magazines, websites, part time coaches, books, parents, friends, and many other potential influences in a student's career, but there is often the most important element in a player's growth missing for our American junior tennis players – and adults for that matter.

Individualized, tailored, one to one environments for giving and receiving the gift of wisdom and experience – this is the true, time-honored process of mentoring. Having a coach that spends time a student on a one on one basis to share experiences, to develop skill sets, to encourage the growth mindset and the growth of a player philosophy, and to push a player to work when he or she needs it. Without this consistently in place, a player has less opportunity for these elements to emerge within his mindset, her knowledge base, his goal setting, or her ability to continue improving.

The term mentor originated in Greek mythology when Mentor, a wise teacher, was asked by his friend Odysseus to watch over his beloved son, Telemachus, as he embarked on a voyage. Mentor gave love, support, and guidance to the child as he grew up until his father returned in the story. Thus, in today's society we have adopted the name mentor into our language and have come to know mentors as those who gently guide and nurture the growth of others during various stages of their development. The best mentors provide valuable, timely feedback through candid conversation (as opposed to military verbal bombardment) to create the proper perspectives. A committed mentor – which any coach and parent should consider themselves – is one that embodies and encourages in their students a range of characteristics.

Mentors embody and encourage *humility*, which is a deep respect in speech and deed when communicating with others, and in sharing wisdom through learning. They exemplify *self-acceptance*, with full awareness of self in body and mind and openly relating to others with confidence. True champions that own this attribute recognize their own shortcomings but also work toward making their weaknesses into areas where they excel. They work to create change and move beyond their own limitations in a humble manner. They believe that they can write their own story, so to speak, that they are in control of their lives and be the author of their own fate.   They symbolize *integrity*, which is wholeness and refinement of character that denote a commitment to personal principles and the ability to recognize and steer clear of tainted influences. Mentors represent *kindness*, which is unconditional love and compassion and a willingness to be open to concerns and understanding.

They personify *trustfulness*, and evoke an inner sense of trust in others and in themselves by having the courage to evolve and the willingness to take responsibility for their actions with clarity and awareness. They show *attentiveness* through deep and honest listening and responding to others whole-heartedly, and in doing so open up opportunities for students to have tangible transformation. Mentors have no problem demonstrating *decisiveness* through their actions with strong emphasis, clarity of thought, and determination to uphold decision-making that comes from the heart.   They epitomize *perseverance* via strength, steadfastness and unwavering determination that embrace and transcend suffering so that eventual success and fulfillment can be rewards. They display *patience* with others, and adapt to their needs through consideration of others. Mentors understand that possessing these qualities is the best way to encourage them in others. As Jerry McClain of Seattle, WA once said, "The best example of leadership is leadership by example."

The Blueprint for Success

Going back to the aforementioned Pyramid of Success from the legendary UCLA Basketball Coach John Wooden – as you can see below – the traits that build toward the pinnacle of success have much to commitment and little to do with talent. Given that basketball is a team sport and tennis is an individual sport unless one is talking about doubles, there can be some varying interpretations from person to person as to how these concepts would relate to tennis. However, given what we've learned from the social learning theory and modeling in the last chapter, it's clear that, when placed in a group setting, students can learn from each other in addition to learning from their coaches – especially when leaders encourage the students to work together in a supportive and cohesive environment.

Without question a good coach will at the very least facilitate the student's capacity to generate enthusiasm and industriousness for the game of tennis, encourage self-control, alertness, and the desire to take initiative in the discovery of new ideas. Certainly the coach's developmental planning and structure will influence a player's ability to have intentness both during matches and practices to achieve both short term and long-term goals of skill acquisition and confidence. Essentially, defining the fundamentals of being and the fundamental life skills that give players the opportunity to achieve competitive greatness is what the Pyramid of Success does. Laying these ideas out in black and white can be helpful – since most students, when given specific assignments and specific things to accomplish – can accomplish what is asked of them.

With Wooden's ideas coupled with the results of Dweck, Ericsson, Gladwell, and others who have both marginalized the importance of talent and outlined similar notions about the personalities of successful people, a blueprint for growing a champion begins to emerge.

A Shared Vision Between Player and Coach

Any owner of a vineyard would tell you that better wine can be produced by the soil being of poor quality. This is because the vines have to "work" harder.

In addition to having the character traits Wooden outlines, tennis players who possess a genuine commitment to the game, a work ethic that not just spans over an extended period of time but also permeates throughout many aspects of their life, self reliance, independence, the desire to constantly perfect fundamentals, performance-based and process-oriented thinking instead outcome-oriented thinking, and the ability to think for themselves and problem-solve, are players who inevitably exhibit more success over time than players who have so-called talent but are missing some or many of these qualities.

College coaches can know the qualities to look for when scouring the globe, identifying and recruiting talent for their programs. Junior Tennis Directors at clubs and academies can use these ideas when deciding whom to scholarship for their clinics to draw other kids. Coaches on court can have a clear idea of what character traits they need to promote to their kids or their pro players or whomever while they teach and refine different skill sets. Parents can raise their children with specific intent and gain a better understanding of how to raise a successful child, regardless of whether or not they play tennis – or any other sport for that matter.

The growth mindset, the science of success – and this Pyramid of Success – all apply to the game of tennis, basketball, and every other sport that exists, but more importantly it applies to relationships, employment, leadership, and life in general. Developing these qualities should be a top priority for parents and coaches alike, and if they are – then developing these qualities will become a top priority for the student.

Attribution theory, originally founded by Fritz Heider in 1944, states in part, that people strive to understand daily events to establish stability for themselves. The types of attribution that athletes – and certainly tennis players included – make for success and failure are strongly related to their emotions. Parents, mentors and coaches can mold the meaning that players assign to their performance and outcome. Coaches and mentors can educate parents on how to do this in the home, but the leaders in a player's life can learn to recognize the athlete's unspoken attributions from the displayed emotional responses. Whether the emotions are worn on the sleeve or hidden, coaches can predict or read the emotional mindset of a player based on their attributions, and based on the meaning that the player places on performance and outcomes.

And a big part of coaching is molding the attributions of a player. Like learning a forehand, a player can learn to prioritize performance over results, enjoyment of the sport, playing the game the right way, embodying sportsmanship, and focusing on the process through an overall outlook of a growth mindset. The meaning a player places on various matches and tournaments throughout their career can be more geared towards the development of personality and athletic prowess instead of the live or die, outcome obsessed, win or nothing attitude.

Creating environments which breed success takes a number of core qualities that must be ingrained within the coach's approach. Seeing the big picture is just as important as implementing day-to-day exercises to build skill sets and fundamentals. Below is a story that embodies this concept.

One day a traveler, walking along a lane, came across three stonecutters working in a quarry. Each was busy cutting a block of stone. Interested to find out what they were working on, he asked the first stonecutter what he was doing.
"I am cutting a stone!" Still no wiser the traveler turned to the second stonecutter and asked him what he was doing. "I am cutting this block of stone to make sure that it's square, and its dimensions are uniform, so that it will fit exactly in its place in a wall."

A bit closer to finding out what the stonecutters were working on but still unclear, the traveler turned to the third stonecutter. He seemed to be the happiest of the three and when asked what he was doing replied: "I am building a cathedral."

As story tells it, clearly defined long term goals are just as vital as immediate short term schooling, and knowing where the execution of short term goals ultimately are taking a student gives both the coach and student peace of mind in regards to the direction of their tennis. In reality, what this really means is how focusing on one particular set of skills for a period of time will contribute to the overall effectiveness of a player's style of play. Furthermore, if the student has some semblance of his or her developmental plan that a coach has laid out, that player will be more likely to be willing to make the sacrifices necessary to get better. That player will be more willing to take a step or two backwards in order to take five steps forward.

*   *   *   *

A good optometrist will tell you that the human eye can distinguish 500 shades of gray. Having patience with students and parents – and sometimes having thick skin in the face of criticism is vital for every coach's success and peace of mind. Establishing discipline within a student and a program, and being fair to everyone certainly are obvious prerequisites to being able to create a sound environment as a coach. Understanding that in every situation, with all clients, students and parents, that there may be shades of gray among judgments, decisions and actions can help a coach be flexible within a disciplined setting and have patience with people.

Having – and showing the commitment to a student's progress has a major impact on a student's progress, as leading by example is perhaps the most powerful method of influence a coach has. Being dedicated means staying the course, so to speak, amidst doubt, uncertainty, and adversity coming from circumstance, oneself, or others. In baseball, pro scouts scour the nation and the globe for what they refer to as "separators" when it comes to talent identification. For player and for coaches though, the main separator is commitment. Commitment is the major ingredient that separates those who break through and achieve personal greatness and reach their potential from those who do not. By showing players and students commitment, coaches can inspire it in others.

Being willing to learn from students is a good way to show and practice this commitment, and keeping everyone involved with the developmental planning and execution of progress can maximize enthusiasm for everyone. Having not just long term planning in place, but also day to day planning in place to develop short term goals is essential in keeping the daily practice and development exciting. And the insatiable promotion of process-oriented thinking and performance-based priorities instead of obsessing with rankings and results are vital aspects of a good coach's proverbial playbook. With the possession and execution of a tangible philosophy that a coach can implement both daily and over longer periods of time – incorporating the player's interests and feedback, a coach can grow with his students and be an effective leader.

*   *   *   *

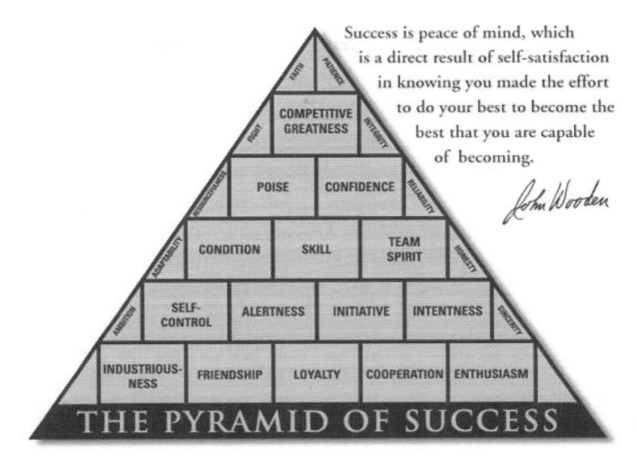

Success is peace of mind, which is a direct result of self-satisfaction in knowing you made the effort to do your best to become the best that you are capable of becoming.

John Wooden

THE PYRAMID OF SUCCESS

Being Taught How to Teach, and Coached How to Coach

If you are a coach, or are considering a coaching career in tennis, let me be the first one to wish you well. Or perhaps I should wish you luck. There are about a million different skills you will need in your profession, ranging from becoming an expert in technique, a seasoned sports psychologist, a leader, a babysitter, a placater, an enforcer, a drill sergeant, a philosopher, and even sometimes a silent observer.

The challenges of learning the tricks of the trade in all the aspects of this game are no different than delving into any other profession. The smarter the people you work with, and the more motivated you are to learn, the more expansive your knowledge base will become. The right information is out there - but you as a coach should seek it out. So if there are a few things you don't know about on a particular stroke - look in the mirror and blame yourself. Ask questions, pursue-pursue-pursue. And pick up a book every once in a while. Any coach who hasn't read Winning Ugly or The Inner Game of Tennis should do themselves and their students a favor and drive immediately to Barnes and Noble.

But of course, knowing something, and being able to communicate that information to someone else can be two different things. The human element is always a challenge, and one that can be rewarding.

In other words, if your player's contact point on his forehand is too late on a regular basis because of improper shoulder rotation, and you are well aware of this - his forehand won't be fixed until he arrives at a place where he is ready to hear your message. That's, of course, assuming you can communicate your message confidently and clearly - which some coaches can do, and many cannot.

We, as players have all been taught how to play this game. So to the coaches of the world reading this, let me ask one simple question: Have you ever been taught how to teach? Have you ever been actually coached on how to coach players?

99% of honest coaches in the US today will say no (or, at least, they will be stretching the truth a bit if they say yes...). In my experience, particularly with young coaches – and unfortunately with many experienced coaches – is that coaches often assume they know everything about the game. I submit that this attitude among coaches hurts tennis in our country, and that we as coaches must constantly possess a desire to learn more about the game from our peers, and particularly from the best players and best coaches in the world. Nobody knows everything, and anyone who thinks they do is naïve.

My father, who is a former college coach and was the Director of Saddlebrook Tennis Academy, preached to his staff in a similar vein. I grew up hearing from him that I was not allowed to coach anybody until we spent a great deal of time together learning the step-by-step methods of teaching proper technique. For him - every stroke in the book has a step-by-step method for teaching beginners. Knowing all of those steps - he said, would enable me to grasp the skills to be able help more advanced players rid themselves of weaknesses, and build up their weapons to greater levels. That, he said, was a starting point to learning the profession.

He told me before I got my first job teaching tennis, "If a coach cannot teach a beginner perfect strokes - strokes that pros would love to have - then that coach has no business teaching good players." Having the opportunity to teach a beginner is very often a much easier task than teaching students with years of bad habits and faulty muscle memory. Can you imagine a math teacher walking into a classroom and seeing the equation $2 + 2 = 5$ scribbled a hundred times on the chalkboard? First the teacher has to erase the incorrect information, and then begin to rewrite the correct information. With beginners, you get a clean slate. All the coach needs to do is provide the right ideas and information and that beginner will have solid fundamentals for a lifetime.

A coach's job is maximizing the talent each student has. If a student can't walk and chew gum, so to speak, then your job as a coach is teach them the same strokes the pros have (in other words, correct technique), and hope - within the context of their ability, that they can eventually keep a few balls in the court. On the flip side, if you have a super human athlete that's a good listener and motivated student of the game, then it's the coach's responsibility that the student develops his game with proper fundamentals and a style of play that is suitable for his body type. So if your super human athlete student who listens well has a great forehand and a bad backhand - yes, that bad backhand is your fault. And yes, you can take a little credit for helping create the huge forehand of his. But don't pat yourself on the back too much for that one stroke - there are several others to get to work on every minute of every practice. That's the great thing about this game - we can all always improve.

As the coach molds the mind of the student, the coach must train the student to know what the coach knows, to think like the coach thinks, and to be self sufficient in a way that allows the student to develop his own personality on the court and his own way of achieving success.

All we can do as coaches is merely facilitate the development of a player. We cannot hit the balls for them, we cannot compete for them, and we cannot think for them. We should not feel like our players should do exactly what we say all the time, nor should we expect our players to be clones of ourselves while on the court. We can only show them the doors – they are the ones that must walk through them.

And even if your student has the most beautiful strokes the world has ever seen - he still has a long way to go in his development because being a good ball-striker and a good player are two very different things. Growing up in Florida, I played at a number of academies down there, and believe me - getting a good practice partner was easy. It seems like everybody has great strokes down there. But there are always a finite number of good players - players that know how to compete, players that can control their emotions - and most importantly, players who know how to set up a point and play smart. I've seen some of the most even-tempered athletic gods walk onto the courts - who also always found a way to consistently go for the wrongs shots and never know it.

Coaches that I respect have talked about this stuff on court about helping the student, have spoken about this over lunch (in between online poker games and Seinfeld episodes), and then we would have meetings after our classes ended and talk about it some more. Our students, what they do well, where they can improve...and you know what I found out from my bosses? They asked just as many questions as I did. But that's what makes them the great coaches that they are. They always want to become a better coach, and they always know that there is something new to be learned. And that it didn't matter if we were working with one of our pros in the top 50 in the world, or one of our juniors in the top 50 in the city - what's right is right when it comes to strokes and shot selection from person to person. And whatever other hindering things the student conjured up - we didn't allow. It was a world of black and white, right and wrong, correct or incorrect, that we created - and our students responded.

The responsibility of the coach is to facilitate constant growth, and we did that to the best of our abilities at the academy. Along the way, no matter how good or bad of a job you do as a coach - there are some students who will love you, some students who will accept your help slowly, and others who would rather you not speak to them about their games.

So what does it take to be a good coach?

It takes a lot of talking shop with people who know more than you do. It also takes knowing who to listen to and what to listen to them about. It takes an open mind as a young coach to learn how to teach the correct technique - to learn all the elements of stroke production and then learn how to instruct the student's body and mind to achieve what's right. It takes an endless pursuit of looking for and finding weaknesses in different players and showing your students how to do the same. It takes a willingness to be open to your student's emotional roller coasters.

It takes good judgment as to what type of personality your student needs in you as their coach to lead them towards improvement. It takes an understanding of what it means to be a leader – and also know how to lead your students toward becoming good people in addition to being good players. It takes knowing that some of your students really do not want your help at all - and being okay with that. Most importantly, it takes showing your players that they can get better - no matter how good they are - and then showing them exactly what they need to do in order to progress.

Some players need a best friend - others need a motivator - and still others a part time coddler and a full time drill sergeant. But most importantly - it takes knowing that you will never know everything - but the confidence in yourself to believe that you might get close with some hard work and a friendly persona.

Goal Setting

Abraham Lincoln once said, "A goal properly set is halfway reached."

S.M.A.R.T. goal setting, according to Dr. Edwin Locke's research in the late 1960's, suggests that setting goals that are Specific, Measurable, Attainable, Relevant, and Time-Bound, lead to enhanced confidence and results. Locke's later work would reveal that goals must have clarity, challenge, commitment, feedback, and task complexity in order to facilitate the most effective outcome. Such goal setting is a significant aspect of understanding where a player was, where a player is, and what a player is going to become.

Setting both short term and long term goals with these ideas in mind can jump-start a player's motivation. Identifying what a player ultimately wants from his or her tennis - whether it's to get a college scholarship, to make it on the pro tour, to be a grand slam champion, to place higher in your league, or simply to win your club championship, can give a player an enhanced sense of purpose both on the practice court and in match play. Once long term goals are set, a series of short term goals can be incrementally put in place over time that provide stepping stones to achieving the ultimate long term goals. By setting in motion clear, achievable, and planned skill sets to learn and improve upon on a weekly basis, a great deal can be accomplished. Without sound goal setting in place, the blueprint for success is incomplete.

Players who suffer from frustration on court and have problems controlling their temperament can resolve these issues and become more positive on court – with an action plan. By simply trying not to be frustrated, the player has no tools to achieve this, no roadmap to get to a more consistently positive emotional state on court, and therefore will likely have little to no success in achieving a new attitude. To say that the player wants to be more mentally tough is a good thing, but will be nearly impossible without a real plan as to how this can happen.

In English pubs, ale is ordered by pints and quarts. So in old England, when customers got unruly, the bartender would yell at them mind their own pints and quarts and settle down. It's where we get the phrase "mind your P's and Q's. On the tennis court, being mentally tough takes a lot more than just minding your P's and Q's. It requires a range of tools – methods of thinking and behaving – skills that can benefit one's tennis but more importantly one's life if implemented on and off the court.

By identifying the times when a player gets frustrated most often and situations where temperament becomes a problem, steps can be taken to rectify it.

Players can set a short-term goal during a week of practice to become hyper aware of their body language in between points. Building on that, during the next week of practice, players can practice solution-focused methods of analyzing how points were played and how strokes were executed. The player can take time during these practices to realize the difference between being his own inner coach instead of being her own inner critic. The following week can be spent on mastering process-oriented thinking instead of outcome-oriented obsession, and the week thereafter could be spent on practicing positive self-talk, where the player builds himself up with encouraging inner dialogue to prepare for the next point. Another week still could be then dedicated to understanding what it means to be fully present in the moment on court, and how often he lingers in the past, dwelling on what could have been instead of focusing on what to do right now.

Each of these outlined short-term goals, which add up to a series of specific tasks that can be focused on from week to week that generate some valuable tools for mental toughness. By incrementally setting clear, tangible goals that a player can likely achieve over short periods of time – especially if she has a coach or mentor guiding the way – long term goals and lofty, broader objectives can be attained.

The same could be said for a player who says, "I want my forehand to be a weapon." By identifying areas of technique where the player excels and areas where he could improve, an action plan can be put into place. Obviously the foundations of the stroke should be addressed first. The player should discuss with her coach the hands – how technically sound his backswing is, contact point, and follow through. Then the shoulder and hip rotation can be evaluated along with the footwork. If more subtle nuances than these foundational principles imply need to be addressed, then short-term goals can be set accordingly. Obviously shot selection and the understanding of offense, defense, and the art of the neutral shot should be considered as well. Regardless of what areas need to be addressed, a specific plan from week to week or even day to day can be set in motion that can build that forehand into a weapon during matches. Practices can be tailored to work on one or two areas of focus that build towards the ultimate goal.

As you can see, both examples of short term and long-term goals listed here are performance related goals. While they may seem like outcome related objectives, arriving at a state of mental toughness, or developing a forehand into a weapon are both far more related to the quality of performance than the outcome of winning or losing. Radio personality Larry Elder once said, "A goal without a plan is just a wish."

Section 2. The X's and O's

It was the famous German architect Ludwig Mies van der Rohe that said "God is in the details." Later the journalist/activist Gloria Steinem said "God may be in the details, but the goddess is in the questions. Once we begin to ask them, there's no turning back."

This section offers the nuances of the game in plain view, showing how the technical and tactical details can help make the game more fun and interesting for anyone. Below is a chart that each chapter in this section will delve into.

Parameters of Technique

Forehand

Grip – Between Eastern And Western	Unit Turn - Rotation	Load with Legs
Backswing – Loop Begins Above the Hand with a Set Wrist	Contact Point – In Front of Body (Semi-Western and Eastern Grips can make contact with a set wrist)	Follow-through over the shoulder (or close to it)
Racquet Head Acceleration	Weight Transfer	Footwork Stance (Open or Closed, or some variation of either)

2 Handed Topspin Backhand

Grip – Bottom Hand Continental (or close to it), and Top Hand Eastern (or close to it)	Load with Legs (open or closed stance, or some variation of either)	Footwork Stance (Open or Closed, or some variation of either)
Backswing – Loop begins Above the Hand with a Set Non Dominant Wrist	Unit Turn	Contact Point – In Front of Body with a Set Non-Dominant Wrist
Top Hand Creating Racquet Head Acceleration	Weight Transfer	Top Hand Guides Follow-through over the shoulder (or close to it)

1-Handed Topspin Backhand

Grip – Eastern (or close to it)	Unit Turn – Sideways Posture Throughout	Load with Legs
Elastic Energy with Chest Expansion, Non Dominant Hand Usage	Backswing – Loop begins Above the Hand with a Set Non Dominant Wrist	Contact Point Out in Front with a Set Wrist (or close to it)
Footwork Stance	Weight Transfer	

Slice Backhand

Grip – Continental (or close to it)	Unit Turn – Sideways Posture Throughout	Open Racquet face
Elastic Energy with Chest Expansion, Non Dominant Hand Usage	Elbow Bent into L Shape on Backswing	Contact Point Out in Front with a Set Wrist (or close to it) and slightly to the side

Forehand Volley

Grip – Continental (or close to it)	Ready Position – Feet and Racquet	Unit Turn	Split Step
Lead/Step with correct foot and push with legs forward	Open Racquet Face	Set Wrist	Arm Swings from Shoulder

Backhand Volley

Grip – Continental (or close to it)	Ready Position – Feet and Racquet	Unit Turn	Split Step
Lead/Step with correct foot and push with legs forward	Open Racquet Face	Set Wrist	Elbow Bent into L Shape on Backswing

Serve

Grip – Continental	Toss Reach up and Location (dependent on the type of serve)	Feet Stance: Pinpoint of Platform	Throwing Motion with Hands
Wrist Snap/Pronation	Unit Turn	Shoulder tilt with hip out	Jump and Landing

The Pro Forehand

The loop, which is a circular motion…

After getting to your back hip with the butt of the racquet facing the ground with a closed racquet face,

- and then reaching comfortably around your hip,
- completing the loop means getting under the ball by dropping the racquet head before swinging forward to strike the ball.
- Starting the loop in ready position by setting, or cocking back the dominant wrist

Clock Analogy:

If the topmost tip of the racquet head were to be facing a clock, then players with good loops

- start with the topmost tips of the racquet head near 12 o'clock. They then move the racquet head around the clock and drop the racquet head to around 5 or 6 o'clock, depending on where the height of the ball is coming toward them.
- Finishing the loop means getting under the ball, where the butt of the racquet points upward to the sky.

Backswing

The Pro Forehand

- Dominant Wrist set, or cocked and locked back during contact

- Elbow in near the ribs

- Racquet out in front of the body on impact

- Racquet face straight, or flush

- Dominant Arm slightly bent

- Hips and Shoulders Open, facing the court

Contact Point

The Pro Forehand

- As the ball approaches, the left foot steps forward toward the ball as backswing begins

- The right foot drags forward during follow through

- Use when opponent's shot is low bouncing

- Use when opponent's shot lands short in the court

The Closed Stance

The Pro Forehand

Positioning of the feet

- Right foot parallel with the baseline

- Entire Right foot firmly planted on the ground in front of the torso

- Left toe planted on the ground behind the torso

- Significant yet comfortable separation between right and left feet create a wide base for good balance

Loading, and Weight Transfer

- To Load is to sit, or bend right knee during backswing, putting all the weight of your body on the right leg, and then stand up or straighten the right leg during contact and follow through

- Body Weight resides more on left foot on follow through

- Use when opponent's shot pulls you wide to the right

- Use when opponent's shot lands deep in the court

- Use when opponent's shot is high bouncing

The Open Stance

The Pro Forehand

- **180 degree Shoulder Turn (or close to it)**
  - Left Shoulder points at the ball as it's (before contact) coming during backswing, and right shoulder points at the ball as it's going (after contact) during follow through.
  - Open Hips on impact

- **During Backswing, sideways posture**
  - Left elbow pointed at the ball (for right handed players)
  - Left shoulder pointed at the ball (for right handed players)
  - Hips and chest face the right side fence of the court (for right handed players)

- **During Contact Point, Hips and Shoulders Face the Court**
  - Specifically, shoulders square up so the chest and hips (ideally) face the shot target on contact

- **During follow through, Right Shoulder points at the ball as it travels toward your opponent**
  - Shoulders turn so chest faces opposite side left doubles sideline

Shoulder and Hip Rotation

The Pro 1-Hander

Load with Legs

Unit Turn With Sideways Posture

Backswing – Loop begins Above the Hand with a Set Non Dominant Wrist

Contact Point Out in Front with a Set Wrist (or close to it)

Elastic Energy with Chest Expansion, Non Dominant Hand Usage

Fundamentals

The Pro Backhand

The loop, which is a circular motion…

After getting to your back hip with the butt of the racquet facing the ground with a closed racquet face,

- and then reaching comfortably around your hip,
- completing the loop means getting under the ball by dropping the racquet head before swinging forward to strike the ball.
- Starting the loop in ready position by setting, or cocking back the non dominant wrist

Clock Analogy:

If the topmost tip of the racquet head were to be facing a clock, then players with good loops

- start with the topmost tips of the racquet head near 12 o'clock. They then move the racquet head around the clock and drop the racquet head to around 5 or 6 o'clock, depending on where the height of the ball is coming toward them.
- Finishing the loop means getting under the ball, where the butt of the racquet points upward to the sky.

Backswing

The Pro Backhand

Left
Hand
Drives
Through
The
Ball

● Top Wrist set, or cocked and locked back during contact

● Non Dominant Elbow in near the ribs

● Racquet out in front of the body on impact

● Racquet face straight, or flush

● Non Dominant Arm slightly bent

● Hips and Shoulders Open, facing the court

Contact Point

The Pro Backhand

- **180 degree Shoulder Turn (or close to it)**
  - o   Right Shoulder points at the ball as it's (before contact) coming during backswing, and Left shoulder points at the ball as it's going (after contact) during follow through.
  - o   Open Hips on impact

- **During Backswing, sideways posture**
  - o   Right shoulder pointed at the ball (for right handed players)
  - o   Hips and chest face the side fence of the court

- **During Contact Point, Hips and Shoulders Face the Court**

- **During follow through, Right Shoulder points at the ball as it travels toward your opponent**
  - o   Shoulders turn so chest faces opposite side doubles sideline

Shoulder and Hip Rotation

The Pro Slice

Unit Turn
With
Sideways
Posture

Open Racquet face

Elbow Bent
into L Shape
on Backswing

Contact Point
Out in Front
with a Set Wrist
(or close to it)
and
slightly to the side

Elastic Energy with Chest Expansion,
Non Dominant Hand Usage

Fundamentals

The Pro Serve

Unit Turn	Load/Pause	Jump	Landing
Toss Reach Up	Platform Stance	Throwing Motion	Follow Through
Pinpoint Stance	Shoulder Tilt	Contact Point	Forward Momentum

Fundamentals

Grip Chart

The Eastern Backhand Grip	The Continental Grip	The Eastern Forehand Grip
Obtained when placing the hand such that the base knuckle of the index finger and heel of the hand are right on the 1st bevel. This is essentially the same as the Western Forehand grip and allows for significant spin and control for one handed topspin backhands.	Obtained when placing the hand such that the base knuckle of the index finger is right on the second bevel. It is naturally obtained when holding the racket as if it were a hammer or an axe, for chopping. Used for the Serve, volleys, overheads, and two-handed backhands.	Obtained when placing the hand such that the base knuckle of the index finger is right on the third bevel. The Eastern Forehand grip allows for more topspin on the forehand while keeping control, because the shift along the handle is only 45 degrees (from the multi-purpose Continental grip).
The Semi-Western Grip	**The Western Grip**	**The Two-Handed Backhand Grip**
Obtained by placing the hand such that the base knuckle of the index finger is right on the fourth bevel. This forehand grip is popular with baseliners who like to hit with much topspin. It gets more hand behind the grip, causing shots to result with more power and spin, and provides a contact point farther out front than a full western grip.	Obtained when placing the hand such that the base knuckle of the index finger is right on the fifth bevel. Compared to the Continental grip, the blade has rotated 135 degrees. This forces the wrist in an uncomfortable twist but allows for the greatest possible spin on forehand ground strokes. This is basically equivalent to the Eastern Backhand grip, except that the same face of the racquet is used to strike the ball. The Western grip facilitates a great deal of topspin.	Obtained by holding the racquet in a regular Continental grip (or close to it), then placing the left hand above holding it in a left-handed Semi-Western Forehand grip (or close to it).

Chapter 4.

Foundations of Technique – Hands and Unit Turn

An Overview

It takes six months to build a Rolls Royce, and thirteen hours to build a Toyota. And when it comes to our tennis games, the same idea is true. When we talk about technique, we must understand that starting with good root concepts can build a solid foundation that can branch out in to more complex intricacies, but these things take time. To ensure that solid foundation, we can start with a few easy concepts to both understand and execute, and then build from there. But high quality strokes take time, energy and thought to construct, just like the Rolls Royce.

The other thing to realize is that while it's totally appropriate to allow different people to perform technique with their own idiosyncratic style, certain elements within a sound technical stroke need to happen. There are certain checkpoints that a player needs to make happen – and how they achieve those checkpoints are up to the player and the person – as long as they take place in the stroke consistently.

The easiest way to teach a player these concepts of technique is through *progressions,* which we will discuss throughout the book.

For our purposes, we can compartmentalize all of the aspects of technique into three main parts: the use of the hands and wrist, the unit turn, and footwork. By knowing these three things and how to execute them within each stroke, you will have a solid foundation in your game and a more than adequate knowledge base about the game. The following segments explore the hands and the unit turn.

This is a teaching made easy chapter, or a technique simplified portion of the book. By starting with these ideas – one can build solid technique much easier. A lot of coaches will point to a million different aspects of technique in order to explain – often laboriously and clumsily, all the million different ways of elucidating this part of that stroke or that part of technique. And while many times these coaches may be relatively logical regarding their explanations of one small thing or another – what this chapter seeks to do is to provide a theory of everything, so to speak – or rather a few straightforward, uncomplicated notions that provide a unified theory of how all strokes work.

This chapter ignores the kinetic chain, elastic energy, momentum and weight transfer, racquet speed, and a great deal of other intriguing explanations about technique. These concepts are valuable and some of them extremely important for the players who possess a real commitment to the game. They, however, are not foundational principles, and are not the building bocks of technique.

*   *   *   *

In February 1878, the first telephone book was published in New Haven, Connecticut. The book was one page long and had fifty names in it.

In a similar vein, the game of tennis has advanced about as much as our phone books have grown in size. With racquet and string technology providing greater opportunities to strike the ball with more spin and power, and newer generations learning from the strengths and weaknesses of their predecessors, the game is played at a higher level now than ever.

A big reason for the game's advancement has been the perfection of skills over generations within the hands and the unit turn, and below we will explore the various checkpoints that take place within every great stroke on the pro tour. While personal style should be considered a good thing, certain things nearly always happen within a fundamentally sound stroke – and below we are going to take a look at some of these checkpoints. With these ideas, a player can have a skeleton in mind that lies beneath the surface of a stroke.

Hands and Unit Turn

In every stroke, whether it is the forehand, backhand, volley, overhead, or serve, *the first two things to know about technique is how you want to turn the shoulders (and hips), and what you want to do with your hands and wrist.*

Each stroke has its own specific, unique methods of turning, and when it comes to using the hands and wrist, all of the best pros in the world operate in almost exactly the same ways. By identifying these common denominators in the strokes of the world's top players, then an understanding about your own game can blossom.

In this segment we will briefly touch on a range of shots that illustrate how the hands – specifically the wrist, and the shoulder turn are the two top priorities in your technique, and for more detailed descriptions the use of these technical elements you can refer to subsequent chapters in the book.

It's important to recognize that some strokes call for shoulder and hip rotation, where the player will turn a full 180 degrees from start to finish – or close to it, and others call for a shoulder turn where once the player has established a sideways (or closed) posture, it must be maintained – and opening up or rotating can be the worst thing one can do.

The same can be said about using the wrist, where on many shots one must cock/lay their wrist up, or *"set" the wrist*, creating a U-shape or V-shape from the knuckles to the lower forearm, with the wrist being the bottom part of that shape – both on the backswing and on contact. Some shots call for the wrist to be set throughout the entirety of the stroke – once it is set – it stays locked, and other shots call for the wrist to be locked until contacting the ball and then relaxed. Others still require the wrist to never be set or locked.

Not paying attention to these things can be detrimental to a player's ability to reach their potential, and it's every coach's responsibility to teach their students how to properly use their wrists and turn their shoulders on each stroke. Below are some simple principles that the pros follow on each stroke.

Topspin Forehand, and Two-Handed Topspin Backhand

The forehand and the two-hander have a lot in common, particularly when it comes to the unit turn, the loop on the backswing, the contact point, and the follow through. Most players with a good two-hander will tell you that the backhand is just a left-handed forehand with the right hand going along for the ride. This is true in two key ways – ideal shoulder rotation on both of these strokes is almost identical, and the use of the wrist is also nearly the same on both sides.

The hands and wrist guide the backswing, initiate contact, and complete the follow through, all of which is also made possible in large part due to shoulder and hip rotation.

On both the forehand and the two-handed topspin backhand, top pros meet the ball on impact with a set and locked wrist (left wrist for the backhand, and locked right wrist for the forehand for right handed players).

So most players set their wrist (again, set the right wrist on the forehand and set the left wrist on the backhand) while taking the racquet back to as to ensure that they will meet the ball with their wrists set and locked on contact, which is a position of strength.

The hands and set wrist are also in charge of taking the racquet back the right way, which means above the hand – that the hands and wrist guide the topmost tip of the racquet head from initially facing the sky (where the butt of the racquet faces the ground), and then reaching back while dropping the racquet head below the ball (where the butt of the racquet faces the sky). This is called a loop because of the circular motion that the racquet creates.

The wrist also guides the follow through over the shoulder, where the wrist relaxes and straightens from the set and locked position as it moves over the other shoulder, where the butt of the racquet faces the sky upon completion of the follow through.

In the same way that the two hander mimics the wrist movement on the forehand, the two hander also copies the shoulder and hip rotation of the forehand. On both strokes a full 180 degree turn (or close to it) is executed by top pros, where players establish a sideways posture while taking the racquet back in preparation for the shot, open up the hips to face their shot target on contacting the ball, and then finish the turn by facing sideways in the opposite direction at which they began. On the forehand for example, right-handed pros will often point their left shoulder at the ball as it approaches and then point their right shoulder at the ball as it travels toward their shot target after following through.

We can see these concepts at work with Agassi, Federer, and Elena Dementieva, who use their hands and wrists and turn their shoulders in a very similar way on both forehand and backhand. Above Dementieva is starting her loop; she sets her right wrist with her shoulders and hips turned sideways, cocking the wrist back on her backswing so she can meet the ball with a cocked and locked wrist on contact, just like Roger shows us above.

Below, Fed shows us again how he must open up his hips to enable him to strike the ball out in front with a locked wrist, and then completes his 180 degree shoulder turn on follow through.

The One Handed Topspin and Slice Backhand

On the slice and the one-handed topspin backhand, the shoulder turn differs from the forehand and two-handed topspin backhand. Both the slice and the one-handed topspin backhand call for players to turn sideways, showing their back shoulder blade to their shot target, pointing their front shoulder at the ball, and then maintain that closed (sideways) posture throughout the entire stroke – particularly with the hips, from preparation to follow through.

Opening up the hips even slightly compromises the contact point, where the closed body positioning allows the player to swing away from his/her body and strike the ball out in front with a straight arm. If the hips open, then the arm will be bent on contact and the player will not be able to achieve any leverage on the ball with his arm and racquet, crippling one's ability to create power, and the bent arm on impact also causes the racquet face to often not be squarely straight on the ball and thus killing one's accuracy.

The wrist should also be set on both the one-handed topspin and slice. Roger Federer sets his wrist on both of these shots, like many other pros with one-handers, and he keeps his wrist locked even after contact during the follow through on the slice backhand, and he relaxes his wrist from the set and locked position after contact on the topspin one-hander. While Fed's wrist guides his racquet under the ball on his topspin backhand, he meets the contact point with a locked wrist as the wrist brushes up the back of the ball to create topspin. The locked wrist also allows him to meet the ball in a position of strength, and also to carve under the ball on his slice.

Volleys

On both the forehand and the backhand volleys, the use of the wrist and a solid unit turn are critical.

The number one rule for any volleyer should be to set the wrist, lock the wrist, and never ever break the wrist for any reason. A set wrist helps create an open racquet face that facilitates a player's ability to hit the volleys with a small amount of under spin and also to hit upwards over the net when shots are low to the ground.

Once the wrist is set, the less it moves the better – regardless of the choice of shot, and pros on tour propel the racquet head forward to the ball with their shoulder on the forehand, keeping the elbow slightly bent, but still and locked throughout the stroke. Pros use the elbow (bent from a ninety degrees angle as the racquet is taken back, and straightened out on contact) and the shoulder to propel the racquet toward the ball on the backhand. A set wrist facilitates an open, stable racquet face. Since the backhand volley is basically an abbreviated version of the slice backhand, many of the same principles of the slice backhand groundstroke apply.

On both forehand and backhand volleys, Federer, like many of the great volleyers of today and of the past, turns slightly sideways and closes his hips a bit to help him meet the volley out in front with his locked wrist. If he were to not turn a little sideways, he would struggle to meet the ball out in front in a consistently similar manner on a regular basis.

The Serve and the Overhead

The Serve and the Overhead are both largely driven by the throwing motion produced by the hands, and no throwing motion is sound without a proper unit turn.

A good throwing motion uses the hands well on the backswing up to the "trophy position", the swing upward to the ball enabling an extended contact point, the wrist snap or pronation, and a sound follow through. A good throwing motion also contains significant, well-timed shoulder rotation.

While many strokes thrive with the wrist set and locked at various moments in the technique, the serve is definitely not one of them. In fact, if the wrist ever does become set and cocked back during a player's service motion – forcing the palm to face upward, creating spin on a kick or slice serve becomes very difficult because the racquet face points away from the ball and away from the court with the wrist set.

Developing a good wrist snap (and pro-nating) on a flat serve becomes even more difficult for the same reason. By keeping the wrist straight (not set, and not too relaxed where the wrist bends too far downward either), players give themselves the best chance to mimic a good throwing motion and allow themselves a better opportunity for the racquet face to meet the ball straight on, mainly because a straight wrist makes it easier to reach the trophy position in the right way.

Letting the wrist flop down can often cause issues with the throwing motion, since for many people it can prevent the throwing hand from getting close to the corresponding ear before reaching up and out to contact (the hand will often go too high or drop too low). In other words, a floppy wrist can prevent a player from reaching the trophy position, where the dominant arm creates an L shape just after the toss goes up, which is an essential checkpoint of a sound throwing motion.

Roddick and Federer keep their wrists straight during their service motions, allowing them an excellent throwing motion.

Knowing how to use the wrist is essential to properly move the racquet face to brush up and across the ball on a kick serve, where the wrist propels the racquet face upward and out to the right for right-handers. The wrist also snaps downward on top of the ball and to the right (pronate) to generate racquet speed and power on a flat serve. Roddick and Federer both use this pronating wrist snap to perfection on their flat serves, and they both use their wrists to brush up and across the ball on their kick serves.

On the kick serve, pros stay closed (sideways) with their shoulders slightly longer than on a flat or slice serve. David Nalbandian, like so many other pros, can brush up and across the ball on his kick serve because of how he keeps his sideways posture prolonged. Players who open up their shoulders too early will not be able to hit the ball as high as they can and out in front, or properly brush up and across the ball.

The same principles for turning the shoulders and the wrist snap for a flat serve can be applied to the overhead, and similar problems will occur with mismanagement of the wrist and the shoulder turn.

* * * * * *

As we can see, the unit turn and how we use the wrist for every shot are the foundations of good technique. The shoulder turn is easy to see in the above pictures, but it would require video to illustrate how the wrist can generate power on a flat serve or spin on a kick or slice. We can see in the picture of John Isner above that he has just hit a flat serve in this picture above, since his racquet face is turned outward – he has just pro-nated.

Misuse of the wrist and an improper unit turn can be recipes for inconsistent results, and paying attention to the execution of these two priorities in the right way can ensure every player's development in a positive direction, regardless of the level that they play.

Chapter 5.

Foundations of Technique: Movement and Footwork

Parameters of Baseline Movement

Recovery	Stance (Open or Closed)	Split Step	Moving to the ball while turned	Anticipation

Technically sound movement from the baseline consists of three parts: being in position for the shot with the feet, anticipation, and movement in between shots (which includes splits steps, moving to the ball while turned, and recovery).

Moving to the ball and recovering after each shot have a great deal to do with one's ability to have good footwork. Having good movement in between shots consists of making a solid split step each time one's opponent makes contact with the ball, turning sideways and running to the ball while preparing to hit a shot, facing front and sidestepping on recovery, and keeping the feet moving – on the toes.

Making a good split step is a simple concept where a player jumps up slightly, both feet leave the ground, and the feet land together, at the same time, around shoulder width apart. The split step gives players the poise to move quickly in each either direction. A well-timed split step is made when a player lands with both feet on the ground just as the opponent makes contact with the ball.

Once the split step is made, a good mover turns sideways and runs to the ball. The sideways posture is a necessary aspect of preparation for all types of ground-strokes, and the act running is the fastest method of movement. This facilitates effortless speed in getting to a shot, makes it easy to take larger or smaller steps when necessary, and enhances a player's preparation.

After hitting a shot, immediate recovery is paramount in preparing for the next shot. If a player plans to stay on the baseline, recovery is best executed by facing front and sidestepping. This allows a player to move in either direction with ease – if a player were to recover with his back turned in one direction, the opponent could hit behind him and retrieving that shot would be extremely difficult.

Finally, keeping the feet continuously moving – when a player stays on her toes, she gives herself the chance to move to the ball, make split steps, and recover with maximum speed and minimum effort. By stopping completely and becoming flat footed, a player has to then restart the engine – costing her time and energy – and then make the necessary footwork adjustments. By staying on the toes and bouncing around in between split steps and during recovery, a player gives herself the best chance to use solid

Open and Closed Stances

When it comes to playing in the backcourt behind the baseline, being in position while hitting shots makes ball striking much easier than being out of position. In this chapter, we will define what "being in position" means, when it comes to your footwork, and then discuss the details of different types of footwork patterns.

Modern schools of thought will tell you that when it comes to your feet, being in position for a ground-stroke translates into one of two options: either you hit your forehand or backhand with an open stance – or some variation of it, or you hit with a closed (square) stance – or some variation of that. We will see shortly why these titles (open and closed) can be deceptive, but let's be clear first what they mean.

The open stance forehand for a right-handed player involves the player positioning his right foot placed forward in front of his/her hip, parallel with the baseline, and his/her left foot dragging behind the torso. Typically, a well-executed open stance forehand includes a deep knee bend with the right leg, commonly called "loading", where the player "takes a seat" with his right leg during the back-swing as the racquet head drops below the ball, and then the player stands up with the right leg and he/she brushes up the back of the ball hitting through the shot. Not every open stance is going to be exactly the same, so leaving room for the natural set up of the shot with these principles in mind allows for different variations to occur, appropriately based on where the shot takes place on the court in relation from where and how quickly the player moves to the shot.

The closed stance (or square stance) on a right handed player's forehand involves both feet directly below a player's shoulders, standing comfortably shoulder width apart, with his entire body lined up sideways. Of course, if the player turns around 180 degrees, he will be in a closed stance position for the backhand. The closed stance shot typically consists of a player stepping forward with the left foot toward the net, and dragging the right foot toward the left foot up after contact.

The most common misconception regarding the open stance is simple. Open stance doesn't mean open. Just because it's entitled "open stance", does not mean that the player's shoulders and hips should be open (or squared up facing the net) as he/she takes the racquet back. Players who shy away from open stance have a limited understanding of proper shoulder and hip rotation. The open stance positioning with a player's feet, in an ideal world of technique, does not change a player's need to turn completely sideways during the loop or back-swing while preparing for a shot, nor does it affect the way a player needs to turn into his contact point. Regardless of whether or not a player chooses to use the open or closed stance during a particular shot, shoulder and hip rotation remain constant and should be executed consistently in the same way no matter which type of footwork is chosen.

Players also need to be aware that the name "closed stance" also has no bearing on shoulder and hip rotation. Even though a player's feet may be closed on a shot, they still must adhere to the rules of how to turn the shoulders and hips through a topspin shot.

Having the feet set solidly in either of these footwork patterns is essential, but these stances be executed in such a way that the player can set up for a shot to strike the ball in between waist or chest level comfortably. The open and closed stances are meant to facilitate the easiest, most natural contact, out in front contact point. A good set stance that is too far away from the ball doesn't do anyone much good.

Weight Transfer

With my students, I refrain sometimes from using these two terms, "open" and "closed" stance, to some students that are just being educated about the unit turn and footwork. Here's why: to achieve best results for a particular shot, there must be some element of weight transfer. Most coaches will tell their students not to move backwards while hitting their shots, which can be good advice, depending on the circumstances, but moving backwards through a shot is infinitely better than not having any momentum or weight transfer move in any direction. In other words, it's better to lean somewhere than to go nowhere.

What the terms open and closed stance promote in some students is a lack of weight transfer in any direction.

I tell my students to step into their shots with one foot or the other. More specifically, being in position for a shot means to step into a forehand (or backhand) with one foot and drag the other foot behind on the ground. On the initial step, bending the knee and loading establishes a good base with the feet and provides balance. After swinging through the shot, the player can then transfer her weight onto the other foot. This way, by literally stepping into a shot, a player is much more likely to have the ability to transfer their weight in some direction.

Also, when the player does step into his/her shot, generally speaking a large step into any shot is better than a small one, since a large step provides a wide base, giving greater balance. Conversely, small steps into a shot subtract from one's ability to remain balanced, but smaller steps, sometimes referred to as "stutter steps", can be useful when a player misjudges a ball traveling toward them. These "stutter steps" can help a player adjust to an unexpected bounce before settling into a wider base, or before stepping into a shot with one foot or another.

Conversely, if a player feels they must arrive at a shot with an open or closed stance, they may fall into the trap of hopping into one of these positions, stopping, and then swinging through their shot with no momentum moving in any direction. The player may hit their shot with an open or closed stance (or some variation of either), but if a player runs toward a ball and jumps into one of these positions instead of stepping in with one foot or another, the player's ability to generate pace will be crippled due to the near impossibility of weight transfer forward, backward, or to the side.

For a right-handed player to achieve a proper open stance, one must step into a forehand with the right foot, drag the left, and complete the stroke. For a closed stance, one must step into a shot with the left foot, drag the right behind, and then execute the stroke.

When to Use the Open and Closed Stances

So when is it appropriate to use the open and closed stances? Well, in short, it depends. But there are very simple rules a player can follow to make his/her life infinitely easier when it comes to making decisions about footwork.

For forehands, most top male ATP touring pros use the open stance almost exclusively unless a ball landing short in the court arrives in a rally. Balls landing with any relative depth at all in the court garner open stance. The reason for this is pretty simple: by stepping into a shot with the outside foot and using an open stance, a player can get to the shot in fewer steps, taking less time and energy, and also recover back to the middle of the court after following through in fewer steps, also saving time and energy. It takes an extra step to use a closed stance to get to a deeper ball, but also takes more steps upon recovery in preparation for another shot thereafter. And with the men hitting their shots with greater pace than ever, due to racquet technology and advanced levels of strength conditioning over the past decade, their footwork must be as efficient as possible in order to track down shots with heavy pace and spins.

So, in other words, save time. Save energy. Hit open stance forehands. Why take five steps to a shot when you can get there in three?

On the other hand, most pros are using the closed stance with greater frequency to hit their backhands, and use the open stance for defensive positions. Right handers in this case would step into the open stance shot with their left foot when they are pushed wide or pushed back deep behind the baseline. The open stance topspin backhand is useful for the same reasons an open stance forehand is useful, but when the open stance backhand is used outside of defensive parameters, it subtracts from one's ability to move forward into the court, and subtracts from one's ability to play offense when shorter balls arrive.

Typically, ATP players with one-handed topspin backhands will use the open stance backhand far more sparingly than players with two-handed backhands. Since the open stance provides a natural positioning for hip rotation two-handers want to rotate their hips and shoulders through the shot and one handers do not. Also, because of this same reason, open stance slice backhands do not exist for ATP players, since the slice backhand requires the same sideways body posture through the shot as a one handed topspin backhand does.

This contrast in open stance backhand frequency can be seen in two of the game's greats today in Roger Federer and Novak Djokovic. Djokovic uses, like many two-handers, the open stance backhand in defensive situations far more than Federer does. Both of these players, however, use the open stance forehand almost all the time unless they are attacking a short ball.

So what are the rules? Being in position means to step into a shot with one foot or the other. Within that idea, open stance forehands are used all the time unless the ball lands short in the court. Closed stance backhands are used exclusively, unless you don't have time to step in with your right foot (for right-handers), or unless you are pulled wide or deep in the court.

By using these rules to your advantage, and knowing the benefits of open and closed stances, you can begin to make your own decisions responsibly with your footwork. You can begin to break these rules - but for your own (hopefully) good reasons from time to time. You can discover that how you move can determine how well you play. You can find out that by simply being in position for your shots, they will get a lot easier. And perhaps most importantly, you can learn how to take fewer steps, literally move less than you have before, and at the same be in better position not only for your shot but also be in better position in the court during your rallies.

Movement In Between Shots

In today's game, people hit with great power and often with lots of spin, which makes movement around the court that much more important. We must move better than players of the past if we are to be in position for our shots, because our opponents are hitting with much greater pace than ever before, due to racquet and string technology, as well as the advancement of fitness and stroke technique.

But what does 'move better' really mean? To put it simply, having good movement is a combination of knowing what it takes to have good footwork, and understanding how to anticipate what type of shot your opponent is going to hit before they strike the ball - and where they are going to hit their shot.

Moving to the ball and recovering after each shot have a great deal to do with one's ability to have good footwork. Having good movement in between shots consists of making a solid split step each time one's opponent makes contact with the ball, turning sideways and running to the ball while preparing to hit a shot, facing front and sidestepping on recovery, and keeping the feet moving – on the toes.

*   *   *   *

Moving to the ball and recovering after each shot have a great deal to do with one's ability to have good footwork. Having good movement in between shots consists of making a solid split step each time one's opponent makes contact with the ball, turning sideways and running to the ball while preparing to hit a shot, facing front and sidestepping on recovery, and keeping the feet moving – on the toes.

Making a good split step is a simple concept where a player jumps up slightly, both feet leave the ground, and the feet land together, at the same time, around shoulder width apart. The split step gives players the poise to move quickly in each either direction. A well-timed split step is made when a player lands with both feet on the ground just as the opponent makes contact with the ball.

Once the split step is made, a good mover turns sideways and runs to the ball. The sideways posture is a necessary aspect of preparation for all types of ground-strokes, and the act running is the fastest method of movement. This facilitates effortless speed in getting to a shot, makes it easy to take larger or smaller steps when necessary, and enhances a player's preparation.

After hitting a shot, immediate recovery is paramount in preparing for the next shot. If a player plans to stay on the baseline, recovery is best executed by facing front and sidestepping. This allows a player to move in either direction with ease – if a player were to recover with his back turned in one direction, the opponent could hit behind him and retrieving that shot would be extremely difficult.

Finally, keeping the feet continuously moving – when a player stays on her toes, she gives herself the chance to move to the ball, make split steps, and recover with maximum speed and minimum effort. By stopping completely and becoming flat footed, a player has to then restart the engine – costing her time and energy – and then make the necessary footwork adjustments. By staying on the toes and bouncing around in between split steps and during recovery, a player gives herself the best chance to use solid footwork patterns.

*   *   *   *

It should be understood than having good foot speed - the ability to run fast and move quickly - does not mean that one has good footwork. I've known plenty of fast sprinters and people that could stop and start quickly that had terrible footwork.

Having good footwork means that a player can consistently get their feet in position for each shot in the best way possible. In other words, on the baseline, a player establishes a clean open stance or a solid closed stance for every shot they hit, and they know when to use either of them at the right times – as we've outlined in this chapter. Both at the net and at the baseline, it means making split steps every time your opponent makes contact with their shots, and then moving to the ball with a unit turn.

Being able to move quickly and run fast can facilitate one's ability to have good footwork, but if one moves quickly to a forehand groundstroke but then doesn't set his feet in a good open stance or closed stance, then his speed in moving to the shot was helpful but it didn't have anything to do with whether or not he could get in the best position with his feet to hit the shot.

Also, using some simple principles about moving to the ball and recovery after the shot can contribute to one's ability to have good footwork.

Simply put, when on the baseline, a player should face front in ready position, hover around the middle of the court behind the baseline, and stay on their toes while awaiting their opponent to hit their shot. Once the opponent hits their shot – and you have made your split step in sync with their contact point – it is best to literally turn your shoulders and run to the ball to get to the shot in the quickest possible manner. This not only allows you to move quickly, but effortlessly as well, and with your shoulders already turned - you are on your way to preparing for your stroke. After running to the ball, setting your feet, and striking your shot, it is then best not to run back to the middle of the court, but rather to face front and sidestep back to the middle on recovery.

The notion of running to the ball allows you to maximize your natural speed on the court, and sidestepping back gives you the ability to move in either direction, regardless of where your opponent hits their next shot. Turning and running back on recovery can give your opponent the chance to hit behind you, and hinders your ability to go back where you just hit your last shot if your opponent hits again to the same area of the court.

Running to the ball before getting in position for the shot also gives you the chance to use bigger strides and take bigger steps while moving to the shot - which enhances your speed in getting there, and also allows for short, small steps to be made easily when necessary.

Most top pros use the method of turning and running to the ball on the baseline, as Federer has so perfected. The notion of taking 7 steps to the ball when you can get there in 3 obviously saves energy over the course of a long match, but taking 3 well timed comfortably bigger steps to a shot can promote a wide base when settling into a closed or open stance forehand/backhand.

But it is necessary at times - often frequently - to use smaller steps as well on certain occasions. I like to call these smaller steps "adjustment steps", because smaller steps are needed when moving to a shot that player is not totally sure where or how it will bounce based on the speed and spin of the shot. The smaller, quicker steps can help a player adjust to where the ball is so he or she can move to where they need to move to allow themselves the best contact point on the shot.

Sometimes the wind will take the ball different places, making harder to judge how to time the footwork needed, sometimes the sun will cause issues, and sometimes players just accidentally misjudge where the heck the ball is going to land or how it will bounce. This happens frequently when your opponent hits a high bouncing shot or one with a great deal of spin as well. When any of these things take place, short, quick, smaller little adjustment steps are needed so the player can adjust the position with their feet on the court before settling into the right position in regards to their footwork (open or closed stance at the baseline, or stepping into a volley with the correct foot).

Anticipation

In today's game, people hit with great power and often with lots of spin, which makes movement around the court that much more important. We must move better than players of the past if we are to be in position for our shots, because our opponents are hitting with much greater pace than ever before, due to racquet and string technology, as well as the advancement of fitness and stroke technique.

But what does 'move better' really mean? To put it simply, having good movement is a combination of knowing what it takes to have good footwork, and understanding how to anticipate what type of shot your opponent is going to hit before they strike the ball - and where they are going to hit their shot.

*   *   *   *

Anticipation is basically predicting the future. Imagine a match that you could play, where your opponent verbally, out loud spoke to you, and literally told you where he was going to hit - and what type of shot/spin - before he actually did it. Wouldn't it be nice if your opponent yelled out "topspin cross court!" before he hit his topspin cross-court shot, and did the same for each subsequent shot selection? That would make your life much easier, and it would make playing your opponent much easier as well. While I'm not suggesting that you become psychic to improve your tennis, I am suggesting that you can look for clues to help you anticipate not only what type of shot your opponent plans to hit before they do so, but also where they are aiming.

So what do you look out for? What clues?

While your opponent may not verbally tell you where he is going to hit his shot - or what type of shot he plans to hit (slice, topspin), he does tell you these things with his body. If you learn to speak the language, or rather learn to read your opponent's body, you can know not only where they plan to hit, but also with what type of spin.

There are three key things to watch in your opponent as they move to the ball in preparation for their shots: where the opponent is on the court, how they turn their shoulders, and how they take their racquet back.

Anticipation: Where the Opponent Is On the Court

The concept often referred to as "reading the ball" involves anticipation based on all three of these ideas of watching your opponent, but largely involves understanding where the opponent is located on the court, and where that player is likely to hit their responding shot in a point based on where you have put them.

In other words, your opponent can be predictable in many situations based on their court positioning. While different players tend to use different shots accordingly, most players have habits that can be discovered. Further, most players also respond in nearly the same way under certain circumstances during a point.

Obvious examples would be, during a point, after pushing an opponent wide in the court and forcing him to play a shot on the run, expecting a short reply either up the middle or down the line. Identifying moments when your opponent is out of position often results in a weaker, shorter reply. Also, hitting a high topspin shot during a baseline exchange that lands deep in the court – that the opponent moves far back behind the baseline to hit – will often yield a similar high topspin response that a player with good anticipation skills would expect.

Players not out of position will go cross court more often than not, since the net is lower and the court is longer, and attack short balls down the line, and having that expectation in general – but being open to looking for patterns and habits of each opponent can go a long way toward using anticipation effectively. There are other examples of this, and many of them are relative to the distinctive nature of the specific opponent.

Anticipation: Watching Your Opponent's Shoulder Turn

Being able to anticipate the type of spin your opponent is about to hit takes the surprise factor away, which allows for better potential preparation for the shot you plan to hit in response to theirs. But also being able to anticipate the pace, and the likely placement of your opponents shot gives you an edge in movement as well, because it allows you to get a head start in moving to the ball.

First of all, to be able to anticipate where your opponent will hit, you need a have good understanding of a proper shoulder turn for ground strokes. Among pros the aspects of turning their shoulders are executed in relatively the same way, so we cannot only learn from them what works well, but also what doesn't. That being said, a good shoulder turn can mean different things for different shots, so the act of learning anticipation can for many people be the act of learning more about technique, for both good mechanics and bad.

A good shoulder turn by your opponent for slice backhands and one-handed topspin backhands for the vast majority of pros on tour, at least for moments when their ideal technique shines through, requires a body posture where the players' hips are perpendicular to the net, or sideways, throughout the entire stroke from preparation to follow through. This posture gives them the best chance to strike the ball out in front. If your opponent executes this well, you can prepare for a better shot that they might hit, perhaps with more pace or speed, and perhaps even with better precision, unfortunately for you.

However, if the player opens up their shoulders too much and faces their hips to the net during impact, they are prone swing across their bodies and hit the ball late, which will cause the ball to change direction - all of which you can pay attention to as your opponent strikes the ball - so you can read where their shot will go before they hit and with what quality it might have.

For forehands and two-handed topspin backhands, a solid - and complete - shoulder turn is one that encompasses nearly 180 degrees, where the player begins with a sideways (chest/hips perpendicular to the net) posture, opens up their hips to face their target while contacting the ball - and then finishes the stroke with the shoulders pointing the opposite direction to which they began. But that phrase - "opens up their hips to face their target while contacting the ball" is the body telling the ball where to go. If a pro on tour - say Gael Monfils for example plans to hit a cross court topspin forehand he will open up his hips to face at the crosscourt direction where he is aiming as he makes contact with the ball, and he will face his hips down the line on impact when he wants to hit down the line.

So by watching Monfils' shoulder and hip rotation - one can see that his body is not just telling the ball where to go - but his body is also telling you where the ball will go. The same is also true for the two handed backhand. Players will open up their hips more on a cross court shot than they will a down the line shot, and observing not only a player's preparation - but also their shoulder and hip turn - can lead a player to having better anticipation skills.

Anticipation: How The Opponent Takes the Racquet Back

While watching the unit turn of your opponent can be an acquired skill, observing how an opponent takes the racquet back is far less complex. The bigger the backswing – the more likely the opponent will hit a shot with more pace and speed. Observing early or late preparation can also be a key method of anticipating the outcome of an opponent's shot as well.

The type of spin your opponent is going to hit is usually pretty easy to see during the backswing as well. If the player takes the racquet back with an open racquet face – likely a slice or under spin shot will be struck. On a backhand, most players with a slice backhand will take the racquet back with the opposite hand on the throat of the racquet, which also gives away their choice of shot as well. A backswing with a closed racquet face – and that looks like a loop – is probably going to be a topspin shot.

Topspin and slice shots are hit with different grips as well. Slices are struck with continental grips (or close to it), while topspin forehands typically fall in between eastern and western grips. Topspin backhand grips are usually eastern for one-handers (or close to it) and contain loops as well, while two handers place both hands on the grip – which gives away their choice to hit with topspin, with an eastern grip with the top hand and a continental grip on the bottom hand. By watching how far a player gets under the ball or how closely they approach the contact point – much can be learned about what is about to happen.

Watching grips can be a tool for looking for and finding some weaknesses in the opponent, which is discussed in the tactics and strategy section.

*   *   *   *

You can have good anticipation skills by developing the eye you have for your opponent, and for the pros on tour. By knowing what to look out for - how they take their racquets back, how they turn their shoulders, and where they are on court, you can begin to put your tarot cards aside and begin predicting the future by learning to read people.

Reading people can be a valuable tool in tennis in a variety of ways, and anticipation is one of them. By reading your opponent in 2 simple ways, you can learn where they aiming, and with what type of spin they plan to use.

Another form of reading people on the court, or rather another form of anticipation would be reading the attitude and the energy of your opponent, which can tell you their patience levels, their ability to physically endure the length of the match, and their anxiety levels regarding different areas of their game. While it's easy to tell if someone is tired by examining their sweating, their body posture while walking between points, and facial expressions, if you look closely you can also tell what areas of the game they are insecure about by paying attention to what they get frustrated about. Some people get frustrated by nearly everything and others only about certain parts of their game - and while this aspect of anticipation and reading people can lead to an entirely different discussion, it's worth noting during this conversation, since we're talking about anticipation. Being able to anticipate your opponents actions during the point can mean a lot of different things, and these aspects - aside from knowing where and what type of shot they plan to hit during a baseline exchange - can be just as useful as the others outlined in this article.

Net Coverage

Parameters of Movement at the Net

Push Forward With Legs During Volleys	Split Step	Follow Your Shots In

If a player feels he have good hands at net, then she possesses 1 more weapon in an arsenal towards making a tennis game complete. But volleying well is only part of being effective at net, and one must learn how to move correctly both while moving from the baseline to the net just as he should move his feet correctly for each volley. I've seen some great volleyers shy away from coming to the net as often as they would have liked because of an inability to track down their opponents' passing shots.

Net coverage is today's game can be easy by carrying out a few very simple, easy to execute concepts. While there are challenges in covering the net properly, any player who pays attention to some simple rules regarding movement and the direction of his approach shot or serve, as well as the implementation of precise footwork on each volley. These elements include pushing forward with the legs on each volley, following the approach shot or volley in toward the net, and making good split steps.

These days, people come to the net a lot less than they used to. That has a lot to do with players hitting the ball harder from the baseline over the past 10 to 20 years, with racquet and string technology more advanced than ever. Players can also hit harder in part because the game is evolving - and there are more great players who have learned from the greats of the past - and improved upon the skills and ideas that tennis' legends of the 20th century have handed down. The game's evolution includes a greater attention to technique - and consequently a greater technical proficiency of stroke production - particularly among baseline ground strokes - among more top juniors and pro players.

Because players can hit the ball with greater pace and accuracy from the baseline, the need to approach the net is growing less and less. Players able to strike the ball with tremendous pace can hit winners from nearly any place on in the court, so often the need to finish off the point at the net is unnecessary. Also, because racquets and the perfected techniques used by all the top pro players of today make it easy to create such profound power and heavy spins, approaching the net is tougher than it ever has been. Baseliners in the contemporary court are more capable now than they ever have been to dip low passing shots with a great deal of spin, or to hit passing shots with bigger power through to the open court. This can make life very difficult for a net rusher who has not perfected a few ideas about net coverage, so now it is more important than ever to understand basic net coverage principles.

All that's meant to say is that coming to the net can be challenging. But it can be a worthwhile challenge, and when executed correctly - coming to the net still can be a smart play, and a percentage play to disrupt your opponent's rhythm and put pressure on them, and also to finish the point. The act of coming to the net forces your opponent to make a quick decision - putting him on the defensive - and you on the offensive. The act of rushing the net puts you on offense - and forces your opponent to react to your movement and your shot.

So what principles should one follow when rushing the net? The good news is - coming to the net behind a serve, or behind a groundstroke, or behind a swinging volley struck behind the service line, or behind any shot for that matter, involves the need to perform the same techniques of footwork.

Follow Your Shot.

After striking a ball from the anywhere behind the service line, the prospective net rusher should quite literally follow his approach shot forward toward the net. If you plan to come to the net, you want to run forward toward the net in exactly the direction at which you hit your shot, following your shot straight to the net, and running toward your shot target after you strike the ball and finish the follow-through of your approach shot. In other words, if you approach cross-court - then run cross-court and towards the net, and if you hit down the line - then run down the line.

By following your approach shot, you put yourself in a position to cut off the angle of your opponent's passing shot. The act of following your approach shot also frees you from the burden of guessing where your opponent might choose to hit his passing shot, and it also fees you from being responsible for covering the line or cross court. Because you are following your shot in, you will be only a couple steps away from nearly any passing shot your opponent chooses. Following your approach – which can be a serve or a groundstroke – puts you in a position to cover everything - and anything your opponent may choose.

Following the approach shot also frees you to hit your approach shot any place in the court that you wish - you don't need to restrict yourself from only approaching cross-court, or only down the line.

Of course, there is an exception to this rule. When a prospective net rusher is standing close to one of the singles sidelines, all of the options discussed above go away. When you are in position for an approach shot near a singles sideline, the only chance you have to cover the net with any proficiency is to hit your approach shot down the line. There is too much court - too much ground to cover - if you are standing near a sideline and then hit your approach shot cross court. If you do choose to do this - you better hit a winner because if you do not - you will probably watch the next shot go by you as you lose the point. But by approaching down the line in this situation, you give yourself a chance to cut off the most angles possible that your opponent has while hitting his passing shot. Of course, on the other side of this proverbial coin, if you are anywhere even close to the middle of the court, you can choose to hit your approach shot anywhere you you want - and you will be able to cover the net - if you follow your approach shot in to the net.

In general, once you follow your approach shot in to the net, you can then focus on executing your footwork for each volley, moving closer and closer to the net after each volley (within reason) - which many coaches refer to as "closing" or "closing off the net". Footwork on volleys typically is very simple - after making a split step - you step into your volley with the opposite foot. These two steps are vital for any volleyer, and without them, volleys can become difficult.

Split Step and Pushing Forward with the Legs

Sampras and Rafter were the last two great pure all court players before Federer arrived on the scene. All three of these men rush the net on a variety of different types of approach shots and serves, and all had - and have - excellent results in large part due to their effective movement at net.

The split step is central to a net rusher's ability to cover the net - and his ability to have time to step into his volley with the opposite foot and strike the ball out in front of his body. Once you follow your approach shot, you will want to make your split step at the very moment your opponent makes contact with his passing shot. The split step involves jumping up a couple inches off the ground with both feet - and then landing with both feet on the ground at the same time, with the feet placed shoulder width apart. This split step puts your body in a position of poise, and enables you to respond to your opponent's passing shot with maximum quickness in any direction - thus granting you the enhanced opportunity to cover the net effectively. While Sampras liked to come in behind his powerful serve, Rafter often came in behind his heavy his low-bouncing slice backhand, but both felt comfortable doing so in large part due to the precision and timing of their split steps, which prepared them to move quickly toward volleys both close and far away in the court.

For a right-handed player, once the split step is executed, then the player steps into the forehand volley with his left foot, or with his right foot on a backhand volley.

If the player pushes forward with both legs through the volley after the split step and initial step into the volley, a greater amount of balance while moving through the shot is achieved. The initial step in to the shot makes the volley much easier to cleanly strike, since it facilitates the unit turn, and pushing through the volley with the legs not further enhances overall balance for the shot but also increases one's ability to follow his or her shot into the net.

Without a good split step timed as the opponent has impacted the ball, the initial step into the volley is difficult to make and very often there is no time to do it, and consequently pushing forward through the volley with the legs becomes impossible as well. The split step frees the net rusher to step in to his volley and push forward with the legs through the volley.

By using these simple ideas – a player has a chance to cover the net well. The player then has the best opportunity to cut off the angle of the opponent's passing shots, be in proper position for each volley - and ultimately be successful at the net.

Sliding on Clay

As a Florida native, I grew up playing mostly on clay courts. Before my father became the director at the well-known Saddlebrook tennis academy north of Tampa, he had his own academy in St. Petersburg at the St. Pete Racquet Club, home of 16 clay courts and only 3 hard courts. It was those green clay courts where I did the bulk of my training in high school, and then when we moved to Saddlebrook I had the privilege of playing both on green and red clay. I was also very lucky to be around some great clay court players during those years. For years I developed my game to flourish on this court service, and I learned that while there are many factors that go into playing good clay court tennis, movement on clay and the ability to slide is a top priority for everyone.

Anyone who has ever watched the French Open knows that sliding on clay is a big factor during the course of the event for all players. But at any level of competition, knowing how to slide is a fundamental that can make playing on clay much easier and more enjoyable. Because their are many more hard courts in the US nationwide than clay, this skill seems to fall by the wayside by many American juniors and adults alike. However, with a little practice and the right ideas about execution, learning to slide on clay can be easy and fun.

I learned how to slide on my mother's kitchen floor running around in my socks. I remember coming home from a practice when I was very young, frustrated about my movement on the dirt. I saw a commercial on tv that was advertising Mr Clean with some woman sliding around on her kitchen floors and I thought, "I should do that", as any young kid would think, right....? Anyway, off I went, to my parent's dismay, and they let me continue only after I explained to them that it would help my tennis game, and only after promising them that I wouldn't break anything.

What ensued was my early development of sliding, which began with the notion of leading with my dominant foot (my right foot), letting my body weight go completely in the direction to which I was running, and dragging my back (left) foot behind. The next day I went out to the courts and, perhaps in the only time in my playing career, I actually asked to do some sprints before beginning practice.

It was during these sprints that I learned once and for all how to slide on clay, and the method was similar to what I had done the night before on our kitchen floor. After starting to run a few steps and gaining momentum, I found I could slide at any time by stepping forward, placing my right foot out in front of my hips flat on the dirt, and leaving my left foot back behind my hips, with only the toe touching the clay. Once my right foot and left toe became planted in the midst of gaining some momentum in one direction, I could slide significant distances on the clay according to how fast I was running before beginning to slide. I also found that putting pressure on the ground with both my right toes (front foot) and left toes (back foot) could serve as a braking system to get myself to stop. After doing a number of repetitions of this, and experimenting how far I could slide and how and when to use the brakes, I felt I was ready to begin experimenting on court during a practice.

Any player can learn to slide on the court, and watching the best pros in the world can be a great tool. We all know Nadal is one of the greatest clay court players of all time, but the way he slides on the dirt has a lot to do with his success. And with the women's game raising its standards every year, more and more women on the WTA Tour are learning to move effectively on clay as well by sliding.

What I began to learn as a young kid was, and what Nadal and so many other great touring pros learned to execute as well, knowing when to slide, with what foot, and how to slide into certain shots.

On the forehand, Nadal, because he plays left-handed, slides into most forehands with his left foot, with his left toes pointing parallel with the baseline, and his right toes dragging back behind his torso, thus enabling him to hit an open stance forehand. Federer, of course, does the same thing, just with his right foot since he's a righty, with his left toes dragging behind. With their front toes parallel to the baseline, each of these French Open Champions are able to prepare for their shots while sliding, because the front toes pointed this way allows them to turn their shoulders sideways while taking their racquets back. If the toes were to point forward toward the net, the hips would face square at the net and the players would be able to turn their shoulders throughout the shot. By adding weight to the front toes during the slide, a player can break (stop the slide) at any time smoothly or abruptly by choice, and a little weight added to the back toes dragging can help the braking system be more accurate too.

Because Federer plays with a one-handed backhand, it is rare that he will hit on clay an open stance backhand. Therefore when sliding into his closed stance backhands, he will also slide with his right foot into the shot, where he again leads with the right foot and drags with the left toe behind. While sliding, Fed points his right toes often at an angle or even parallel to the baseline to ensure the shoulder turn that we just discussed before with the forehand.

Federer certainly is more than capable, just as three-time French Open Champ Gustavo Kuerton was, of sliding into an open stance backhand, and I've seen both of them do it with nothing short of excellence. But for any one-handed player, sliding into a closed stance backhand is more common because this makes it easier maintain the proper sideways shoulder and hip posture through the completion of the stroke. This rare shot is and was executed by these players by sliding into the shot with the left foot in front of the torso, again with the left toes parallel to the baseline, and with the right toes behind dragging.

Nadal of course, with his two-handed backhand, will do the same thing essentially on a closed stance backhand, just the reverse again because he's a lefty. By leading with the left foot and dragging behind with the right toe as he slides into the shot, he can execute a closed stance backhand. However, because he possesses a two-handed backhand, he has the option of sliding into an open-stance backhand at any time.

Two-handed players should all learn to slide with both feet on their backhands like Nadal does, because it frees up the ability to hit open stance. If a player only knows how to slide by leading with the dominant foot, mobility becomes limited because the open stance backhand is not possible without being able to slide by leading with the opposite foot. Nadal can slide into his backhand by leading with his right foot and dragging behind with his left toes to hit an open stance backhand, or he can slide with his dominant left foot into a closed stance backhand, giving him options.

I have played against players that knew how to slide beautifully with their dominant foot, but could not slide at all with their non-dominant foot - and consequently I knew that they could not hit an open stance backhand. If they cannot hit that shot, then hitting wide to their backhand is a great play because they will be forced into a closed stance situation off the court, and will not be able to recover back to the middle of the court behind the baseline very quickly or easily.

It's important to understand is that, for the majority of the time, the pros mentioned above slide before hitting their shot. Sometimes players are forced to slide after the shot when they are rushed, or put in a tough situation, or hitting what they believe will be the last shot of the point (one way or another). Sliding on clay enables players to comfortably track down shots during points far away from them on the court, and also enable quick recovery back to the middle in between shots. If a player slides after hitting a shot, they will often be sliding away from the court, making for a more difficult recovery back to the middle of the court and it will often put them out position to win or stay in the point.

Forehands and backhands from behind the baseline, as described above, are obviously not the only shots that pros will slide into before hitting. Any time a player needs to run across the court or move across part of the court before hitting a shot, sliding is appropriate - which can occur mid-court, behind the baseline, or at the net. Good clay court players slide on almost every shot during a hard fought point when forced to move a great deal around the court, and without sliding into their shots before hitting them, their balance and ability to make quick stops and starts in different directions would be unstable at best.

What's also important to consider is the specific clay court one is playing on, since many clay courts are composed of different amounts of clay, which can affect how far and easily one can slide, and how often. For example, if a court is only thinly covered with clay (often at clubs with poor maintenance standards) on the entire court or in certain areas, sliding will be difficult and if one can slide at all it will be limited. On the other hand, courts will plenty of clay and a soft feel to the ground will allow players to slide easily and at significant distances across the court with enough momentum generated before the slide.

The overall moisture of the clay also effects how far and easily one can slide as well. A wet court provides players with shorter sliding distances and less slippery conditions, while a drier court will provide players with potentially longer and easier sliding opportunities but more slippery conditions.

The moisture is also affected by the type of watering system in place at the tennis facility where the clay courts are. Some clay courts have sprinkling systems that water the courts periodically throughout the day, while other newer facilities have underground watering systems. Many of the underground watering systems provide an evenly and well-moisturized court, but also typically create a more slippery surface that makes for sliding and movement comparable to when sprinkler-system courts are drier.

The type of clay also plays a role into how a player slides, since there is a significant difference between playing on and sliding on green and red clay. With both surfaces, all of the general outlined principles still apply in the same way, but there differences are worth noting. Red clay poses more emphatic differences as already mentioned between dry and wet conditions, while green clay often poses more subtle differences. So in other words, red clay will be a more compact and harder surface when it is wet than green clay, making for sliding opportunities on the red clay to be shorter and more abrupt, and players will literally not be able to slide as far or as much when the red clay gets very wet and muddy. Red clay will also be more slippery when it is dry than green clay, and players will then have a greater need to slide and greater opportunities to slide further distances.

Typically red clay, with all things being equal, is a more slippery surface in general than green clay, thus making sliding that much more important while moving around the court. However, like I said, when it gets wet, the red clay becomes far from slippery and sliding becomes not only more difficult when on the run, but also players can slide a much smaller distance into their shots before striking the ball.

Generally speaking, if a player can move well on red clay, he can move well on green clay, and vice versa. By using the concepts outlined above, players cannot only learn to move well on the dirt, but they can learn to enjoy it. The feeling of sliding across the court and hitting a good shot is addictive, and in my opinion there is no better feeling in our sport. Knowing how to move well on clay is a tremendous advantage over your opponent, and being able to use either foot in leading your slides can add to that advantage.

Chapter 6.

Using Progressions to Teach Mechanics and Develop Instincts

Teaching such technique to players doesn't need to be a difficult, time-consuming process if done the right way with good communication between player and coach. By teaching them through the use of progressions, a player can walk before they run, and jog before they sprint, and then learn to sprint with purpose and strategy, and finally enter a race where strategy is involved and implemented.

The basis of using progressions starts with the notion of tossing a player balls out of the hand in the first series of drills, then feeding them static shots with the racquet in the second series of drills, then third putting them into motion with live hitting via controlled rallies, and finally throwing them into relatively unpredictable circumstances with point play.

There are progressions that can teach movement, tactics, and technique all at once, but progressions exist to emphasize one or two skills at a time so as to maximize the effectiveness of the series of drills.

Here's an example of a progressive series of drills that could be the outline for an hour private or semi-private lesson, where two players work on their forehands...

1) Toss out of the hand: The Up and Back Drill

    a. Coach stands on singles sideline near service line, and tosses a short ball for the student to attack, and then immediately afterwards in rhythm tosses a deep ball that pushes the player back behind the baseline.

    b. Tactical Instinct Development: Offense – attacking the short ball and move up to take it early, and Defense – moving back to hit higher over the net, with more arc, more shape to the shot, and more topspin and less pace.

    c. Movement Instinct Development: Moving to the ball while turned, forward and backward movement to allow a waist level contact point (or close to it).

    d. Main Purpose to Discuss between Coach and Player: Technique with Hands and Unit Turn.

2) Feed with Racquet: 3-Ball Drill. Coach is on the other side on court, in between service line and baseline. Coach feeds slightly deep shot to forehand side of student, and then in rhythm feeds another shot to forehand side, and then a third shorter ball shaded toward backhand side.

a. Ball 1: Player hits higher and deeper cross court

b. Ball 2: Player hits and angle off the court cross court

c. Ball 3: Player runs around backhand to hit inside out forehand on the rise to coach's backhand corner

d. Tactical Instinct Development: Student learns how to use forehand to set up the point and open up the court

e. Movement Instinct Development: Player learns side-to-side movement, and where to expect the ball to come back based on shot selection.

f. Main Purpose to Discuss Between Coach and Player: Technique with Hands and Unit Turn. Emphasize Split Steps from player on Coach's contact.

3) Live Ball Rallying: Players hit while standing in No Man's Land, or in between service line and baseline. They rally with controlled, lightly paced shots with ball control emphasized so as to make the execution of technique easier to focus on.

4) Live Ball Rallying: Players hit for consistency cross-court, baseline to baseline. After the tenth shot, players can take a short ball down the line (and then start a new rally).

a. Coach: Monitor hands, feet, and decisions with emphasis on hands and unit turn.

5) Cross Court Baseline Points: Players can only hit cross-court – game played to 11.

a. Coach feeds to player 1, who begins behind the baseline on forehand side. Player 1 hits feed cross-court to player 2, who is on the other side of court behind the baseline, and then they play out the point. All shots must be hit cross-court within the singles lines or else they lose the point.

6) Full Court Baseline Points

a. Coach feeds to player 1, who begins behind the baseline on forehand side. Player 1 hits feed cross-court to player 2, who is on the other side of court behind the baseline on the forehand side, and then they play out the point – except this time they can play within the whole singles court.

b. Coach to emphasize use of the forehand during point play.

The progression outlined above can last up to an hour, and really can develop the stroke production, movement, and tactical instincts of a player if the series of drills is ran in a high energy, attentive way by the coach and players. If the coach focuses on the hands and unit turn, as this particular progression outlines, then the technique will be at the forefront of the player's mindset as they go through the drills.

However, in so doing, they will also receive some ancillary benefits of habit creation through the tactical and movement components of the exercises, especially if the coach interjects quick reminders in this regard that demand basic fundamentals like split steps and good shot selection to the players as they can go through the drills in an obvious, very brief manner. Instinct development takes place through the coach inserting short comments within the scope ongoing conversation about other unrelated material, which for many can be the most profound methods of learning.

This version of a progression for the forehand increases the difficulty of drills steadily over time to allow the player the best chance to perfect what they are working on. Technique development can take place within the context of other skills being naturally advanced. Of course, there are many ways of organizing progressions, and the example outlined above is just one possible option.

There are progressions that can incorporate any number of strokes and situations that provide technical, tactical, and movement development. A two-handed backhand progression, for example, could include the coach first tossing the student from up close some left handed forehands, then feeding with the racquet some swinging two handed topspin volleys, Then, after using the backhand within some full court racquet feeding drills with both forehand and backhand, the final progression could be live full court baseline drills that include both side to side and up and back movement as well as some tactical decision-making reinforcement.

*   *   *   *

Progressions are about making things very easy, and then making things kind of easy, then making things a little bit tougher, and then re-releasing your students into the wild by throwing them back into live ball rallies and point play in hopes of having them incorporate the new things they've learned in a fully realistic situation.

Expecting students to be able to learn new skills and execute them well in a fully realistic situation right away would be a wild, out of control notion without first giving the player a chance through controlled exercises that develop specific skills. If a player has a poor contact point because said student has a limited unit turn and does not set his wrist during the backswing, then throwing him into a live rally from the baseline during a lesson right off the bat seems a bit overly ambitious. By isolating parts of the stroke through progressions with limited difficulty that work up to increasing levels of complexity, the student can have a better chance to evolve.

Chapter 7.

Mirrored Ground-Strokes – Forehand and Two-Handed Backhand

Everyone has his or her own idiosyncratic style of technique. We are allowed that. But within our own style of executing the right concepts with our technique, we can begin to define our own ideal set of principles. As mentioned previously, there are certain things that have to happen throughout a stroke, and knowing those things can take a player a long way toward technical efficiency.

All of the great forehands and two-handed backhands on the pro tour have a great deal in common, and each of the players with these strokes achieves certain checkpoints within the scope of their stroke. For example, the contact points are all pretty much the same, the shoulder rotation, the follow through, etc.

However, because the best two-handed backhands in the world are basically opposite-handed forehands with the bottom hand on the grip along for the ride throughout the stroke, there is an opportunity for players to have virtually identical technique on both forehand and backhand. By having the same backswing on each side, this is possible since the shoulder and hip rotation and contact points on forehand and backhand are so similar. A forehand and a two-handed backhand call for a very similar unit turn – that is to say that both strokes call for rotation of the shoulders and hips.

Not every great pro has the exact same backswing loop on their forehand, and the same could be said about pro backhands. The loop, which is a circular backswing that promotes a non-stop, continuous fluid backswing, enables a great deal of power since it makes it easier for players to have a swing that never stops – and the momentum generated from the loop facilitates greater racquet speed. That doesn't mean a loop is perfect for every player out there - but in this case, we will talk about how having a loop on both forehand and backhand can make a player's life a little easier.

The most efficient loops for both two-handed backhands and forehands begin the wrist being set in ready position (top hand on the backhand), and the unit turn takes place in conjunction with the beginning of the loop. On the forehand, the dominant hand takes the racquet back with the wrist locked, and the elbow pointing toward the ground. If the elbow starts to get to high – going out away from the body – the loop takes longer to complete and therefore there has wasted motion and effort. The elbow will be in – relatively near the ribs on contact – so why take it out and place the elbow high and away from the body at any point of the backswing?

There really is no good answer to this question. There are some pros that are good enough athletes and have fast enough hands and can get away with it – but that's just it – they get away with it – it doesn't help them in any way and occasionally hurts them. Some would say that extending the elbow up and out higher on the backswing creates a larger backswing and can help generate more racquet speed – the argument that the bigger the backswing, the faster one can accelerate through the ball. However, using the legs, shoulder and hip rotation, momentum and weight transfer, and body strength can generate plenty of racquet speed. The backswing is only a small part of how racquet speed can be generated, and ensuring a solid contact point is more important than swinging really fast.

At the same token, the racquet face on the backswing, if the wrist is set properly, yields a closed racquet face throughout the loop. Not setting the wrist or closing the face during the loop of a topspin forehand or two-handed backhand can cause an open racquet face on contact and cause the shot to fly upward more than intended. Players accidentally miss long quite often when this mistake occurs.

On a right-handed player, the same of course could be said about the left wrist and the left elbow during the loop on the backhand. By generating the same circular motion during the backswing loop on both forehand and the two-handed backhand, the strokes are easier to maintain over time because they are basically the same stroke. A player can solve problems on one side by simply referring to what they do on the other side, and little discoveries that facilitate better ball striking on one side can be applied to other side as well.

Teaching and learning can be made easier when mirrored strokes are used. Because, in general, most good coaches today will teach the forehand to beginners and intermediate players first – learning the backhand can become a fast and easy process for the teacher to teach and the player to learn – if they use what they learned about the forehand and apply the same concepts to their backhand. Through a series of progressions, players that learn how to use their dominant hand and wrist and how to turn their shoulders on their forehands can simply apply the same concepts to the other side. Nearly everything they learn on the forehand they are actually learning also for their backhand, so the learning process is accelerated.

The backhand is best taught by teaching the player an opposite handed forehand in a series of progressions, and then putting on the other hand on the grip for a realistic true two-hander.

The following elements of technique are almost identical on the forehand and two-handed backhand: shoulder rotation, use of the wrist (top hand/non-dominant hand on the backhand), getting under the ball, contact point, follow through, and footwork.

The last element – footwork – needs some qualification. Most pros will hit predominantly closed stance (a.k.a. square stance) on the backhand unless pushed backwards or wide in the court, while they will use open stance or some variation of it far more frequently on the forehand than they will the two-hander. There are further explanations regarding some of the footwork differences and variations between forehand and backhand in later chapters of this book. The point is, though, that the execution of the open and closed stances on both forehand and backhand is very similar when it comes to weight transfer, foot positioning, load with the legs, and so on.

Below is a sequence study of Rafael Nadal's forehand, which shows the loop on his forehand. He begins by setting his wrist, with the butt of the racquet facing the ground in ready position. Then, after he turns sideways, he brings his racquet – still in the same position – near his back hip. This is when the circular motion described above begins as he reaches back behind his hip and drops his racquet head – pointing the butt of his racquet toward the sky before propelling his strings toward the ball and striking it out in front of his body.

Nadal's loop, like so may other pros, helps him generate a smooth yet powerful stroke. I like to tell my students to imagine a clock, with the topmost tip of their racquet head starting at noon when the loop begins, and then the player must circle around the clock down to 5 or 6 o'clock before swinging forward toward the ball.

Power Sources for Ground Strokes

Leverage	Unit Turn/Rotation	Racquet Head Acceleration
Load with Legs	Weight Transfer	Elastic Energy

Having great mechanics and technique can give a player tremendous power. We can identify and prioritize certain elements of technique in our strokes to generate more and more power. Racquet speed, the use of the legs, shoulder and hip rotation, leverage, and forward momentum all work simultaneously throughout the execution of a well-struck forehand, and all contribute to one's ability to create power and hit the ball harder. Also, as we will see in the next chapter, elastic energy is a significant power source as well for the forehand.

Racquet Speed

The first and most obvious way to hit the ball harder is to increase your racquet speed. In other words, swing your racquet faster when hitting your shot.

These days, having a good loop during the backswing contributes to the ability to swing faster through the shot. A good loop involves the player, where the backswing begins above the hand, holding the racquet up (with the butt of the racquet facing the ground). With the topmost tip of the racquet starting at 12 o'clock – and then circling around the proverbial clock down to 5 or 6 o'clock before swinging low to high up through the ball. Having a loop makes it easier for players to have a long, continuous motion with the stroke.

In addition to the loop, the follow through also contributes to racquet speed. Having a full, complete follow through allows a player hitting a forehand to maximize racquet speed. After contacting the ball out in front, a good follow through entails finishing the stroke with the racquet head over the shoulder or near the left ear (for a right handed player), with the butt of the racquet facing up to the sky. By accelerating on the follow through, enhanced racquet speed can occur.

Loading with the Legs

The legs are one of the strongest areas of the body. Depending on the stance, by bending the knees during the backswing and standing up as the player brushes up on contact, the legs generate an added momentum and force into the shot.

Open stance ground strokes are best hit by "loading" with the outside leg (for a right hander) during the backswing, and then standing up on contact. Of course, on a closed or square stance ground strokes, both legs load and then lift up on contact and follow through.

Shoulder and Hip Rotation

The unit turn on the forehand and two handed backhand is a significant power source and a major foundation of technique. Typically, what pros on tour will do in regards t the unit turn, is rotate their hips and shoulders 180 degrees or close to it.

After turning sideways to the ball during the backswing, pros rotate and open up their torso, facing the net, when they make contact. After making contact out in front of the body, pros rotate their shoulders and hips even further, to the point where they face sideways in the opposite direction at which they begin. So right handed pros point the left shoulder at the ball as it coming toward them before contact, and then point their right shoulder at the ball as it's going after they hit the shot and follow through. This rotation not only facilitates an out in front of the body contact point, which adds power, but also helps the player use his or her entire body to hit the forehand, and thus this unit turn is a major power source.

Leverage

As mentioned, contacting the ball out in front of the body adds a considerable amount of power to a forehand and a two hander, especially when compared to making contact more to the side of the body or behind it.

As a basic principle in physics states that leverage is an action, power, or force of a lever – in our case it's our racquet and our dominant arm. The longer the lever, the more power a player can get. By extending out and striking the ball far out in front of the body, a player can maximize her own leverage and thus dramatically enhance his ability to generate power. By contrast, hitting the ball in close to the body, with the dominant arm bent in an L shape, with the player creating little to no leverage, and has no extension out in front of the body, he will struggle to generate the amount of power that she is capable of.

Weight Transfer and Momentum

Another major power source is weight transfer and momentum. A forehand or two hander that contains a sound transfer of body weight from one foot to another is a shot that uses more of the body to hit the shot in a well-balanced way, and the act of transferring the body weight creates body momentum into the shot.

Right-handed pros place all the weight in the body onto the right foot during the backswing of a forehand, for example, and then finish the stroke with all the weight on the left leg on the follow through. The act of transferring the body weight in this way facilitates forward momentum when leaning into the shot, and also allows for the body weight to go completely in one direction or another when forward momentum isn't appropriate. On very deep shots or balls landing wide in the court, it is sometimes more suitable for a player to transfer the weight backwards slightly or more to the side, but regardless the act of transferring the weight and creating body momentum in the best direction for the situation can add a great deal of power to a player's forehand and two hander.

*   *   *   *

By using all the power sources available adding the ability to hit ground strokes with more effortless pace can be a great benefit to players of all sizes, shapes, and abilities. Loading, rotating, hitting out in front, transferring the weight, and accelerating with the racquet head all are foundational principles of forehand technique, and all add power to the stroke.

Chapter 8.

The opposite hand on the forehand

Most people think that when a right-handed player hits a forehand, the right hand and arm are doing all the work in the stroke.

The right hand and arm take the racquet back (usually ATP pros use a loop), the right hand and arm create the swing by dropping the racquet head below the ball and brushing up the back of and through the ball, and then of course the right hand and arm finish the stroke with a follow-through someplace over the opposite shoulder.

And that's it, right? Well, not quite.

All of the above-mentioned pieces of the stroke are vital. But the positioning of the wrist of the dominant hand (within the context of the take-back, the swing forward, out and up, and the follow-through) is only part of what top ATP pros have been doing for years.

The 2nd (and equally if not more important) foundation of the forehand topspin stroke is shoulder and hip rotation. I tell my students that are still learning the basics of technique that working on their stroke means two things: understanding how to position their wrist throughout the stroke, and understanding how they want to turn their shoulders and hips during the stroke. Putting movement aside in this conversation, the unit turn is one of the building blocks of technique, as we've discussed at length already in this book.

And this is true for all strokes, especially the 21st century forehand. Before we delve into why the opposite hand on the forehand is a major foundational element in technique, we first must understand what proper shoulder and hip rotation means.

The vast majority of the best forehands on the pro tour today have nearly identical shoulder and hip rotation, and when analyzed closely, Roger Federer and Andre Agassi, for example - and most others - execute their forehands by turning their shoulders and hips 180 degrees. As these players with classic forehands take their racquets back above the hand, they all achieve a sideways posture, often with their back shoulder blade visible to their shot targets, facing in a perpendicular stance to where they are aiming their shot. These players all then open up their hips on impacting the ball with grace and elegance, facing their belly button directly at where they plan to hit, and then once the follow-through is completed their chest is facing the opposite direction to which it began. Facing one way (sideways) at the start, facing front upon contact, and facing the other way (sideways opposite) at the end of the stroke.

McEnroe and Connors used to the do the same thing, turn the same way, but after watching them for years, one can wonder if they just wanted to see both sides of the crowd before and after each stroke...Ha! But really, these two legends of the 1970's had almost identical shoulder and hip rotation as our top pros today possess, the main difference in technique being the absence of a loop as they took the racquet back in the days of old, as well as modern players far more often not only having a loop, but a more pronounced follow through over the shoulder - where the butt of the racquet faces the sky at the end of the follow - through in an effort to generate more topspin. By understanding what it means to turn correctly, we can understand not just why the greats of today strike the ball with such ease and effectiveness, but why most top pros throughout the history of the game hit their forehands well.

So if the above ideas are understood, and a player wants to always achieve this proper shoulder and hip rotation on all forehands, then a right-handed player may consider using his left hand to facilitate this process (and a lefty his right hand). Each of the above-mentioned modern pros (Federer and Agassi) uses their left hand with great agility and effectiveness to help them turn on their forehands. As they take back their racquets when preparing for a forehand, their left arms are up and out in front of the body, as if by either pointing the elbow or the palm at the ball as it approaches toward them to strike. The left arm points in the same direction as the sideways chest faces in the beginning of the stroke.

Then, to enhance the hip turning into contact and thereafter, to facilitate the entire rotation, the left arm can be pulled across the body. Dmitri Tursunov, a top 20 ATP pro from Russia, and protege of my former boss (and current ATP Touring Coach), Vitaly Gorin, uses his left arm to enable his shoulder and hip rotation on all forehands - especially when put into difficult or defensive positions. By pulling the left arm across the body after initially pointing his elbow at the ball as it approaches his zone of contact, he is able to turn completely and correctly throughout his entire stroke with ease, and he also creates an additional power source for his forehand. The act of pulling his left arm across his body generates an elastic energy that not just enhances the unit turn rotation, but also can help increase racquet speed acceleration through the ball.

Without an awareness of the opposite arm on the forehand, rotation can be stunted, or abbreviated. By leaving the left arm on or near the torso throughout the entire swing, rotation is often stifled because the left arm is literally in the way and prevents players from turning all the way. The opposite hand in this case hangs like a giant dead fish from a player's body, not moving, and not allowing anything else to move. By not turning properly, contact points and wrist positioning will often be compromised, and so will accuracy and power.

Additionally, one is far better off, when preparing for a forehand, to keep the left arm either straight or slightly bent, with the elbow pointing relatively upward. If the arm is bent and the elbow is pointed downward, creating a V-shape with the arm and elbow, shoulder and hip rotation can also be negatively affected. With the elbow pointed down, the left arm can inhibit rotation - and with the elbow facing straight at the ball or even upward, a player can more easily pull his left arm/hand across his body and therefore turn more completely.

For beginners, I have my pupils just learning the game using their opposite hands without them knowing it. After they literally point with their finger at the ball as it approaches them, I then tell them to catch their racquet once their follow through has finished. This idea of catching the racquet after the follow through really is not advisable for advanced players who wish to vary their levels of acceleration a great deal. Catching can shorten a follow-through and unintentionally inhibit acceleration. But if the student is made aware that catching their follow through is only a temporary method of creating an awareness for them as to how to use their left arm (or how to get it out of the way) to enable good rotation, then they will begin to understand quickly what they need to do. Catching used in this way - as a temporary method - can useful in these isolated circumstances.

More advanced players that are exposed to this information for the first time tend to latch on to the ideas of pointing their opposite hand's elbow at the ball as it approaches, or pointing their opposite hand's palm at the ball, before they pull their opposite arm across their bodies to help them turn more effectively.

So the next time you're thinking about how to turn on your forehand, think about how your opposite hand and arm can help you. Try pointing your elbow or palm at the ball as it flies though the air toward you - and then pull your non-dominant hand across your body. It could make the difference between good technique and something else, and a good shot or a bad one.

Chapter 9.

The 1 Handed Backhand

The 1 handed backhand can be separated into two different shot selection choices: a slice backhand or a one-handed topspin backhand. Developing both of these shots for 1 handed players is essential for a player to reach his or her potential. Even for players who use a two handed topspin backhand, adding a 1 handed slice backhand into the arsenal adds a great deal of variety to one's game and also can enhance technique on the backhand volley, since both shots call for similar technique.

The Slice Backhand

Even in today's tennis game, with power tennis and heavy topspin becoming increasingly popular and widespread, the slice backhand can be just as effective as ever. The slice, or "chip" – or also known as "under-spin backhand" - can be an effective weapon for any player when executed correctly. The slice backhand can be used in a variety of ways - as an offensive tool, a defensive maneuver, or even as a change of pace and spin that can surprise an opponent.

When it comes to understanding the technique of every shot that exists in tennis – like we talked about in the opening chapters - what any player must first know are two simple things: how to turn (shoulders and hips), and how to use the hands and wrist. And of course, the slice backhand is no different - these two elements are the two main ingredients for developing a reliable slice. All of the other elements of technique, while vital to the success of the shot, support these two top priorities.

To understand the unit turn on the slice, you must allow yourself to possess the notion that the slice backhand is a one-handed backhand. Any and all one-handed backhands require the ball-striker to posture the body sideways, with the chest and belly-button facing 90 degrees from the shot target, by showing the back shoulder blade to the shot target. This posture should be established not only during preparation for the shot, but shall also be maintained throughout the entire course of the swing and follow-through. While it can be occasionally permissible for the shoulders to slightly open up - to begin to slightly face more towards the net, it is paramount to keep the hips closed - or sideways throughout the entire stroke.

Executing this idea can be challenging for players with two-handed backhands, who are accustomed (or should be) to opening up their shoulders and hips upon impacting the ball. Not opening up is often a difficult habit to create for them, but one that needs to be developed over time.

The positioning of the wrist throughout the slice is equally essential as learning the unit turn. I use the terminology "set the wrist", "lock the wrist", or establish a "U-shape" with your wrist. They all mean the same thing - to take a continental grip (or close to it) and lift up the wrist to where you can literally see a shape that looks like the letter U created by the back of your palm, your wrist and the top of your forearm. By laying your wrist back in this way, you put yourself in a position of strength when contacting the ball.

There's no question that Roger Federer has the one of best slice backhands in the game today. But Andy Murray has a great slice too - and both players have a great deal in common with their technique. Both players set their wrist as they take their racquets back during preparation for their shot, and they keep their wrists set and in a locked position throughout the stroke. Their wrists are set so much that during the backswing - as they wrap their racquets behind their necks - their strings almost touch their hair (their racquet frames would do so if their wrists were not set). The backs of their hands face their left ears.

Both Federer and Murray value their wrists staying locked throughout the stroke so much so that both players use a substantial follow-through to give themselves added insurance to help themselves maintain their wrist positioning. Both players swing through the ball and afterwards follow through up above their contact, with their racquet faces facing them. This follow through not only helps the players maintain their locked wrist, but also lengthens the stroke providing a longer, smoother swing.

The long, smooth swing is another important element to consider during the slice, since most topspin shots involve a great deal of acceleration of the racquet head. Power is primarily generated by Murray and Federer on the slice by stepping forward into the shot, creating forward momentum - which allows them to decrease racquet speed while still achieving a certain amount of pace on their shot. Power is also achieved through the leverage they get by contacting ball out in front with a straight arm, which becomes possible only with a maintained sideways posture and a locked wrist. But the slice is never ideally used as a major method of power during a point, and always used by top pros as a shot to set up the point as opposed to finishing.

Getting back to the backswing - both Murray and Federer take their racquets back with a bent and relaxed right elbow (on their dominant hand). Their right elbows are so bent and relaxed that often a 90 degree angle can be seen from shoulder to wrist on their right arms. This is worth mentioning - because players that take their racquets back with a straight - stiff arm - often struggle with executing their slice - and keeping their dominant arm straight often lends itself to a stiff, short, jerky stroke. By bending the dominant elbow on the backswing into an L shape, a square or rectangular shaped area between the dominant arm and the chest is created.

Also, to perfect the backswing of the slice backhand, one must consider that - ideally - one vital goal is to swing as straight through as possible. We all hear the low to high advice from coaches on topspin shots, but on the slice it's a little different. Obviously, to generate the amount of under-spin desired on any slice backhand - one needs to take your racquet back in varying levels above the ball, and swing in varying levels downward to cut under the ball (before following through up above contact!), thus creating the spin. But the more straight through the swing can be – relatively speaking - the more accuracy and reliability can be achieved. And the backswing has everything to do with how straight through you can swing. By simply taking the racquet back at or only slightly above wherever the level of the ball is, swinging relatively straight through the slice is natural.

On the other side of the coin - the last thing a player wants to do is take the racquet back the same way on every slice. If the ball is low - by your ankles or knees - and the racquet is taken back around the neck – a player has no choice but to chop downward at the ball. This chopping downward either causes the slice to float (too much spin - too little pace) - or the shot will be missed in the net. But by taking the racquet back lower when the ball is lower - and higher when the incoming ball is higher – a player provides himself with the easy opportunity of having a relatively straight through swing on your slice.

The use of the opposite hand on the slice is also important. While Federer and Murray possess different idiosyncrasies in their slice backhand technique - both of them achieve of all the basic fundamentals we've discussed thus far. Both players also use their left hands to add stability and strength to their slices. While Federer holds the throat of his racquet with his left hand and Murray holds near the bottom of the throat and top of his grip, both players use their left hands on the racquet in a very similar way. Both players hold on to the throat or grip with their left hand as they swing forward toward the ball - and then they let go - and only then does the shot become executed by one hand. Both men propel the racquet forwards with the left hand on the throat, and then let go.

After letting go with the left hand, both Murray and Federer pull the left hand back behind the body, expanding their chests out and squeezing their back shoulder blades together in a comfortable but powerful way. The elastic energy created by this a significant power source – by helping generate racquet speed, and also helps the players maintain the proper unit turn/sideways posture.

The slice backhand, once a player has mastered these fundamentals of technique, can open many doors and create a wide range of opportunities during a point. The ability to change the speed, pace, and spin during a point can throw off even the best players in the world. The slice provides chances to exploit extreme western grips used by opponents, and can be a productive way to rush the net on approach shots. The slow, heavy slice when players are off the court can take the place of a defensive lob to allow a player time to recover back to the middle of the court when pushed back and/or wide in the court. The slice can also be a great method of purposely bringing your opponent into the net.

Ultimately, the slice backhand is an essential tool in the proverbial toolkit of shot selection. Once a player masters how to turn, what to do with the wrist, and a few other simple concepts, he or she can not only develop into a more complete player, but also begin to employ a wider range of strategies than before. Oh, and did I mention that it feels like a million bucks when you hit a slice backhand well?

The 1 Handed Topspin Backhand: Parameters of Technique

Grip – Eastern (or close to it)	Unit Turn – Sideways Posture Throughout	Load with Legs
Non Dominant Hand Usage Creates Elastic Energy with Chest Expansion	Backswing – Loop begins Above the Hand with a Set Non Dominant Wrist	Contact Point Out in Front with a Set Wrist (or close to it), extended arm
Footwork Stance	Weight Transfer	Follow Through with Racquet Head Above the Chest

The one-handed topspin backhand, like all shots, is hit best when certain elements of technique are executed. Nearly all pros on tour who have the best one-handers in the world have a great deal in common with their technique. While the strokes of many pros may look different to the naked eye, pros with the best one-handers make certain things happen consistently within the scope of their shot making. Federer may have a different look to his topspin backhand than his countryman Stan Warwrinka, just as Gustavo Kuerton's technical style differed from that of Tommy Haas.

Of course, there is room for personal style, and how a player makes these elements of technique happen throughout the course of the stroke, then he or she has the best chance of hitting a clean, well-struck shot with maximum effectiveness and efficiency. These elements entail, as all strokes do, the use of the hands, the unit turn, and the feet. These three components of technique are interconnected, and the better that one is performed, the more likely the other parts are to be also efficiently carried out.

Above is a chart that outlines the parameters of technique for the one-hander, and expresses how the hands, unit turn, and feet are performed.

Hands

The *backswing* for forehands and two-handed backhands, where a loop is made, (beginning with the racquet taken back above the hand with a set wrist, and a circular motion is made to facilitate fluid continuous swings), is not different in those respects for the one-handed topspin backhand. Using an *eastern backhand grip* for the shot (or close to it), pros that hit a one-handed topspin backhand can use a *loop* to help them create racquet speed, get under the ball, and brush up on contact to create topspin.

Like the slice backhand, the *non-dominant hand* holds onto the throat of the racquet, and, after the loop finishes and the racquet begins to swing forward toward the ball, the top hand can be a power source for the shot. By pulling the left hand back behind the body, both shoulders can also pull backward during contact. This forces the chest to expand, both shoulder blades to squeeze in toward each other, creating *elastic energy* that can increase racquet speed, and because of this can give the player more effortless power. Expanding the chest, like on the slice backhand, forces the back shoulder blades to squeeze together, and while enhancing power in the shot, can also facilitate a better unit turn by helping the player keep the hips closed from backswing to follow through.

Unit Turn

As mentioned in the foundations of technique chapter, the one handed backhand calls for a unit turn that specifically requires a *sideways posture* throughout the stroke, where the player faces perpendicular to the net.

Using an eastern grip makes keeping a strong wrist through the shot far more possible, where continental and western grips force a player to meet the ball with a weaker wrist position. Because only one hand remains on the grip as the ball is contacted, keeping a firm wrist through contact as the player brushes up the back of the ball and generates topspin is paramount. Many players who use the eastern backhand grip imagine themselves pointing the butt cap (or bottom of the grip) at the ball after completing the loop on the backswing before swinging forward to strike the shot, and this helps them keep a firm, set wrist.

This grip not only allows for an easier time maintaining a *strong wrist through contact*, but also – as long as the hips stay closed – allows for maximum leverage. If the *hips stay closed*, a good loop is made, and the right grip is used, then players can brush up the back of the ball on contact with a straight arm, hitting as far out in front of the body as they can comfortably reach. Once the player has made contact with an extended arm, if the racquet head *follows through upward above chest level*, maximum acceleration and overall smoothness of the swing can be had.

Feet

Most pros use a closed, or square *stance* on the vast majority of one-handed topspin backhands, regardless of whether or not they choose a slice or topspin shot. *Loading with the legs* on a closed stance one handed backhand is not different than loading on a two handed backhand, where the knees bend during the loop, and the player stands up while brushing up to create upward force for added power and balance.

There are occasions where players with elite one handers use an open stance when pushed wide in the court, but because using the open stance makes it difficult to maintain the sideways posture throughout the stroke, the open stance is used sparingly. The open stance makes it easy to open up the hips which can compromise the contact point integrity, and therefore accuracy and power.

However, when pushed back deep in the court, it is common for pros to step backward with the outside foot and load with the outside leg, in order to get into the best possible position for the shot. Often after loading with the back leg, pros that possess great one-handers hop up with the back foot and then land on the same foot in order to help keep their hips closed and emphasize the load with the legs to generate more power.

*   *   *   *

Many people feel that the one handed backhand is becoming an increasingly obsolete shot as the game continues to evolve, and as all players hit with more power each year. However, the evidence suggests otherwise in the cases of players like Justin Henin, Richard Gasquet, and of course, Roger Federer – and there are plenty of other examples that could also be named. If a one handed player possesses sound technique, the one handed backhand can be just as effective – if not more effective – than any two handed backhand.

Chapter 10.

The Two-Handed Topspin Backhand

Grip – Bottom Hand Continental (or close to it), and Top Hand Eastern (or close to it)	Load with Legs (open or closed stance, or some variation of either)	Footwork Stance (Open or Closed, or some variation of either)
Backswing – Loop begins Above the Hand with a Set Non Dominant Wrist	Unit Turn	Contact Point – In Front of Body with a Set Non-Dominant Wrist
Top Hand Creating Racquet Head Acceleration	Weight Transfer	Top Hand Guides Follow-through over the shoulder (or close to it)

In every stroke, certain things have to happen for the shot to be hit in a technically sound way. While every shot is best hit with a certain amount of idiosyncratic personally preferred style, each stroke has a number of elements that must occur for the shot to be hit with maximum efficiency. The two-handed backhand is no different.

While many of the top pros on tour (who posses the best two handed backhands in the world) have different ways of achieving these technical check points, they all find a way to consistently execute these elements of technique.

Above is a chart that outlines the elements that take place among every great two-handed backhand in the world on the pro tour. The grip, how players use the legs and feet to generate weight transfer and get in position, the use of the top hand, and the unit turn all are necessary parts to technically sound two-hander. How players choose to make these things is up to them – and as long as they do, they are likely to have the best two-hander that they are capable of having.

Grip

By using an eastern grip with the top hand (or close to it), and a continental grip with the bottom hand (or close to it), with the hands held together on the grip, a player has the ability to hit relatively flat or with heavy topspin. If either hand moves too far away from either of these parameters, a player may become less versatile, and may limit the ability to either drive through the ball or create spin, or both.

Loop

Many pros have different types of backswings, but all great two handers on the pro tour have a loop at some point in their backswing. A loop is a circular motion that begins with racquet head above the hand, where the racquet creates a C shape before swing forward toward the ball. Many pros create this loop in a variety of ways that work for them, but by setting the wrist of the top hand, the player is more likely to make contact in a position of strength with the non-dominant wrist set on impact.

The loop starts with the butt of the racquet facing the ground, and upon finishing the C shape, and as the player begins to swing forward toward the ball, the butt of the racquet faces the sky. In so doing, the player has created fluid racquet head momentum, kinetic energy, and continuous movement that resulted with a dropped racquet head under the ball. This loop prepares the player to accelerate upward through the shot.

Top Hand Creates Racquet Head Acceleration

The two handed backhand is a top handed dominated stroke. The top hand drives through the ball on contact, and it is the top hand that creates the racquet head acceleration through the shot. With the top hand generating the racquet head speed, a player provides himself with the best opportunity to extend the hand out in front of the body on contact, hit with effortless power and vastly increased accuracy. If the bottom hand is used too much to create acceleration, the hands tend to pull in and across the body while swinging toward the ball, causing a jammed contact point that too close to the body or late, or outside the strike zone.

Load with Legs

Whether settling into a closed (square) stance or an open stance, loading with the legs is a vital element of technique. The act of loading, simply put, is bending the knees during the loop of the backswing, and then standing up with the legs as the player accelerates up through the ball. This thrusting upward with the legs not only provides a player with great balance, but also provides a significant power source.

Unit Turn

The unit turn for the two-handed backhand is very comparable to the unit turn for the forehand. Upon achieving a sideways posture during the backswing, the shoulders and hips begin to open up and face the net during contact, and the body continues to rotate further on follow through, resulting in the chest facing the opposite direction at the end of the stroke in which it began. This 180 degree shoulder and hip rotation (or close to it) facilitates an out in front contact point, racquet speed, and provides a significant power source by getting the whole body moving into the shot.

Weight Transfer

During the loop, a great two hander will place all or most of the weight of his body onto the outside foot, and then transfer all of that body weight to the inside foot during the follow through. Ideally, this weight transfer takes place on both closed (square) and open stance backhands. In so doing, a player can get all of her weight going into the shot. Weight transfer is an important aspect of footwork, and can also facilitate the execution of the unit turn rotation.

Footwork Stance

A player can put himself in the best possible position to hit the two hander by planting the feet into a solid open or closed stance. The closed stance is hit most often, while open stance is used for more defensive positions, like when a player is pushed wide or very deep in the court.

The closed or square stance is executed by stepping forward toward the ball with the dominant foot before striking the shot, and dragging the back foot forward after striking the shot. Both feet have the toes facing the sideline, and the most efficient closed stances contain loading with the legs and weight transfer.

The open stance is performed by stepping out with the outside foot, with the toes parallel to the baseline, while the dominant foot drags behind the torso during the backswing. A good open stance calls for a player to load with the outside leg, and transfer the body weight to the dominant foot on follow through.

Contact Point Out in Front of the Body

Making contact with the ball out in front of the body, with the dominant elbow in relatively close to the ribs, is arguably the most important parameter of technique. By striking the ball with the hands comfortably extended out in front of the waist or the chest, and the non-dominant wrist set (or cocked back), a player can meet the ball in a position of strength.

All of the other parameters of technique exist mainly to aid in a player's ability to make contact out in front, so knowing the exact ideal contact point for the two-handed backhand is paramount for a player.

Follow Through Over the Shoulder (or close to it)

Just as the top hand generates the acceleration through the ball on contact, the top hand guides the follow through over the shoulder as well. By finishing the follow through over the shoulder, a player completes a range of motion throughout the shot that completes a long, fluid, effortless swing that enhances power and racquet head speed. At the end of the follow through over the shoulder, the butt of the racquet should faces the sky, and the frame of the of the racquet should be able to scratch a player's back or back shoulder.

Chapter 11.

The Forehand Volley

"I believe that a simple and unassuming manner of life is best for everyone, best both for the body and the mind," said Albert Einstein.

When it comes to the forehand volley, keeping it simple with your technique has some major advantages. With today's game becoming more and more about power, and with players increasingly capable of hitting with more pace and more topspin from the baseline, it is more important than ever to have a simple, concise, and effective technique when approaching the net.

Having a good forehand volley can mean a lot of things from person to person, but in this article we will discuss how some of the best volleyers our game has seen in the past decade or so execute their technique. By seeing what they have in common, we can identify the elements of technique they employ in order improve the efficiency of our forehand volleys.

When it comes to the technique of the forehand volley, there is a little more to it than blocking the ball and hitting it out in front. Simply put, knowing the grip, how to turn, knowing what to do with your wrist and your arm, and having a good notion of footwork, the forehand volley can be a reliable, powerful, and accurate shot for each of us.

To start, let's discuss the grip. All pros use a *continental grip* (or very close to it) for their forehand volley – for all volleys for that matter. The continental grip frees up a player's ability to hit all types of volleys, regardless of how high or low a player must reach to hit the volley. When the volley is low, near the ground, using a continental grip makes it easy to strike the ball with an open racquet face, and on all other volleys - if they are high (above the chest) - or waist level - the continental grip makes it easy for players to strike the bottom of the ball - creating a little slice or under-spin.

Ideally, the greatest volleyers in the world look to hit a little bit of slice on each forehand volley, and this grip makes it easy. Players of the past like Rod Laver and John McEnroe used this grip when they approached the net, as well as recent dominant forces like Roger Federer and Pete Sampras. Eastern or western grips make it increasingly difficult to hit the bottom of the ball to hit slice and also to have an open racquet face without compromising the right wrist position.

To be clear, we can define an open racquet face as holding the racquet so that the side of the strings that will soon strike the ball face slightly upward to the sky. Grips other than continental tend to point the racquet face straight or even downward toward the ground, making the task of hitting the volley over the net pretty tough, particularly on low volleys.

The forehand volley's elements of technique, as outlined above, are all interconnected as you can imagine. When one thing is missing, other elements can suffer. On the other side of the coin, when some elements are well executed, other elements can become easier to execute. That is why we are, in this chapter, approaching the forehand volley in as holistic manner as possible.

With that in mind, we can say that a good *shoulder turn* can benefit other elements of technique. By hitting the forehand volley with a *slightly sideways posture*, keeping the wrist of the dominant hand cocked up, achieving what I and other coaches call a "*set wrist*", while contacting the ball. By meeting the ball on the forehand volley with a set wrist - players can make contact with their shot in a position of strength. That's why a big rule at the net is to set the wrist at all times - and keep it locked in that position. If the wrist straightens out, players meet the ball with a weaker position, not as strong to handle shots hit with a lot of pace by the opponents. Also a locked wrist stabilizes the racquet face, enabling players to meet the ball the same way consistently from shot to shot. The unlocked wrist destabilizes racquet face control, allows the racquet face to point in a number of different directions, which negatively affects ball control.

Patrick Rafter, as he approached the net during his great career, came to the net each time able to make contact with his forehand volley out in front with a locked wrist.

On the forehand volley, once the wrist is set and locked in ready position, the wrist should stay locked throughout the stroke. To ensure the best possible ball control, keeping the wrist locked even after contact for a brief moment - essentially pointing the racquet face at the target - allows for a consistent way to facilitate accuracy and have a well-tailored finish to the shot. In finishing the stroke by pointing the racquet face at the target, players will end up with the butt of their racquet facing 90 degrees to their left (for right handers). If a player finishes with their racquet face pointed far to the left or right, they risk breaking losing control of their shot and even breaking the wrist.

When the player, while hitting a forehand volley, positions their torso and chest in a slightly sideways posture, the wrist can be set with a contact point out in front. Players don't need to turn a full 90 degrees to be completely sideways, but a 30 or 45-degree turn is enough. If the player remains totally open and faces the chest front (toward the net), hitting the ball out in front with a locked wrist become very difficult, and players who do this are likely to hit the ball late, to the side, and/or with a flimsy wrist.

As for the dominant arm, this is what controls the swing. Now, some people say not to swing on your volleys. Well, that's not really true - there's got to be some swing - for the racquet to generate any pace on the shot and to make contact out in front. The arm should be slightly bent at the elbow, and relatively frozen and locked in that slightly bent elbow position. We want the arm - with the elbow not bending very much at all back and forth - to swing from the shoulder like a pendulum. This way, the swing can be a significant part of the technique but it will remain simple and concise.

The shoulder takes the arm out away from the body to take the racquet back a few inches, and the shoulder swings the arm - still remaining slightly bent - forward to hit the ball out in front - bringing the elbow in on contact. The elbow goes out away from the torso while taking the racquet back, and then comes in close to the ribs to make contact. With the elbow out on impact - hitting the ball out in front becomes difficult or impossible, but when the elbow is in (right elbow near the right ribs for right handed players) on contact - it's more natural to make contact more out in front.

Of course, the harder one's opponent hits, the less time the net player will have to perform the pendulum-like swing from the shoulder. So the harder the opponent hits, the shorter the swing should be. On the flip side, when the opponent hits a shot that floats, a bit bigger swing can be more useful so the net player can generate his or her own pace. This concept allows players to hit their forehand volley by using their opponent's pace - and also have the ability to create their own pace when they need to.

By keeping the arm still in the slightly bent position - all this is possible. But if the arm swings back and forth from the elbow, it becomes more difficult to hit volleys out in front with a locked wrist. And as the slightly bent arm propels forward toward the ball before impact, the arm should swing the racquet forward at a slightly downward angle when the ball is near chest of waist level - but not too far downward. By swinging slightly downward with a locked wrist and an open racquet face, it's easy to hit the bottom of the ball, creating a small amount of slice or under-spin. On high volleys, swinging downward more is needed to hit the ball down into the court, and on low volleys - the arm should swing slightly upward so the player can hit the volley up over the net. Pete Sampras was a master at digging out low volleys when he came in behind his serve, and this was in part due to the way he punched his low forehand volleys with a slightly upward motion.

When it comes to *the feet*, keeping it simple and concise allows you time to hit good volleys. Generally, once a split step is made, right-handed pros will step into their forehand volleys with the left foot. Making a split step means to hop up a little bit off the ground with both feet, landing with both feet on the ground at the same moment and at the same time the opponent makes contact with their shot. The *split step* gives players the ability to be poised and move in the either direction quickly to hit a volley, and also allows time for the player to step into the volley with the correct foot - in this case the left foot for the forehand volley. Without the split step - *stepping into the forehand volley with the left foot* suddenly becomes difficult because there often is not enough time to do so when the opponent hits a passing shot with pace. Stepping forward with the left foot on the forehand volley not only helps players turn their shoulders the way they should, but it also gives players forward momentum on their volleys - which gives them added power and balance.

I tell my students to step forward and 30 or 45 degrees to the right, which typically means that they step toward the ball as it approaches them. On some occasions, when the opponent's shot flies through the air straight at the net player, they can step a bit to the side with the left foot while hitting the forehand volley instead of forward and a little to the side.

After leading with the left foot, moving through the volley and pushing forward with the legs give an added power source of forward momentum, it facilitates the act of following the shot in to close off the net – cutting off the angles of the opponent when they attempt passing shots, and creates added balance with the body.

Mardy Fish likes to come in to the net throughout the course of his matches with relative frequency - often behind his powerful ground-strokes as well as behind his big serve - and each time he does - making a split step allows him a good chance to step into his forehand volley with his left foot. He knows that being in position with his feet on his forehand volley is just as important as using his hands the right way. Max Miryni, one of the few true serve and volley players left on the pro tour, also has a great split step to compliment his well rounded net game and reliable, concise forehand volley.

In summary, after making a split step upon the opponent's contact, hitting a forehand volley entails propelling the slightly bent arm forward with a locked wrist and an open racquet face, while stepping into the shot with the left foot and then pushing forward with the legs.

Having a reliable forehand volley means using these elements of technique in a concise manner. By mastering these relatively simple parts of the forehand volley, you too can have a forehand volley like the pros.

Chapter 12.

The Backhand Volley

While the majority of the best players in the world play more often from the baseline these days, using traditional volleys at the net still can be an effective way to pressure your opponents and finish points. I say traditional volleys, because swinging topspin volleys are becoming increasingly common in today's game, and that's not what we are going to focus on in this chapter.

The backhand volley, which can be considered similar in technique to the backhand slice groundstroke, is an essential tool for any player that wants to be proficient at the net. Most pros on the ATP Tour that possess the best backhand volleys on tour have a great deal in common in regards to the technique of their stroke. We can identify these elements to help us improve our own backhand volley. These elements include 1) how to use the wrist and the elbow of the dominant hand, 2) how to use the opposite hand, 3) how to turn the shoulders, and 4) how to move the feet.

This notion of stepping into the shot is relatively simple, since it should be the goal of every player to make a split step and *step into their backhand volleys with the right foot* (for a right-handed player). Once a player leads with the right foot on the backhand volley, pushing forward with the legs and moving through the shot enhances the contact point, balance, and the ability to cover the net, as discussed in the last chapter on the forehand volley.

Before all volleys (and before stepping into the backhand volley with the right foot), a net player will want to *make a split-step*, and after the split step he or she should want to step into the shot with the correct foot. This split-step is made by jumping with both feet up off the ground an inch or two and then landing with both feet on the ground simultaneously, shoulder-width apart. Both feet should land on the ground at the same time a net player's opponent makes contact with their shot, thus completing the split step. Typically, the absence of a good split step, or a split step that is not in sync with the opponent's contact point will lead to an inability to step into the backhand volley with the right foot, which is an essential piece of the backhand volley technique. The split step adds balance to all volleys and makes it infinitely easier for the forward-moving player to cover the net.

A good step into the backhand volley with the right foot can positively influence the *shoulder turn* of the shot, which is also pretty easy to execute. By simply *turning sideways* (a comfortable amount), a player hitting a backhand volley instantly has the ability to make contact with the shot out in front and a little bit to the side with a relatively straight arm. Of course, hitting the ball out in front enhances both power and accuracy, and by turning a bit sideways, pointing the right shoulder towards the shot target, this happens more naturally on the backhand volley.

The correct use of *the opposite hand* adds strength and stability to the backhand volley. While the vast majority of good backhand volleys on the pro tour are considered 'one-handed backhand volleys', which is what is being discussed in this article, both hands are involved in the stroke. For a right-handed player, the fingers on the left hand should be wrapped around the throat of the racquet both in ready position at the net, and during the take-back during preparation for the backhand volley shot. After the take back – which will be discussed shortly, the left hand holds on to the throat of the racquet even as the racquet propels forward toward contacting the ball, and then the hands separate before impact.

By holding on to the throat with the left hand as the racquet moves forward toward the ball before impact, you can ensure that there will be more strength and stability with your the backhand volley. Tommy Haas has excellent technique across the board with his backhand volley, and he uses his left hand this way, and of course the same could be said about Justine Henin before she retired. After letting go with the left hand, both of these players expand their chest and squeeze their back shoulder blades together, creating an elastic energy that generates enhanced racquet speed in a very similar way as the slice backhand ground stroke.

The use of the wrist is obviously one of the most essential piece of the puzzle for any volley (forehand or backhand). The rule is to *set and lock the wrist*, and to never break it ever for any reason. Ever. The set and/or locked wrist of the dominant hand (meaning to tilt the wrist up to create a U or V shape from the knuckles to the lower forearm) can provide the volleyer a positioning of strength to the net player that a broken wrist cannot provide. The set and locked wrist also provides a chance for the net player to point their racquet face at the shot target while contacting the ball out in front.

Once the wrist is set and locked, which should occur during ready position and be held throughout the backhand volley, the use of the elbow in the dominant arm is the last element of technique to consider. After setting the wrist, making the split step, and turning sideways, the volleyer should bend the elbow into an L-shape while taking the racquet back, bringing the racquet face behind the player's head or back shoulder. Then the volleyer should straighten the arm/elbow as he or she propels the racquet toward the ball just before making contact. So the elbow is bent on take back, and straightened on impact as the player moves through the volley and pushes forward with the legs.

After impacting the ball with a slightly open racquet face, thus hitting the bottom of the ball, most pros with great backhand volleys have a small follow-through upward, pointing the racquet face up to the sky to ensure that their wrist stays locked. Patrick Rafter used to do this on his backhand volley with regularity.

So as we can see, locking the wrist, using the opposite hand, turning a little sideways, and the act of bending and then straightening the elbow in conjunction with proper footwork are the all-encompassing elements of good technique on the backhand volley of the pros.

Chapter 13.

The Ideal Service Motion

No longer do pros survive on tour with one great weapon - they must be at the very least efficient in all areas of the game just to be able to compete. And regardless of your level of play, as the game continues to evolve - you must grow with the times and develop your style and technique as you get older if you want to compete successfully.

As the game becomes more and more about power with vastly improving racquet technology (among other factors), correspondingly the serve rises in importance. While the serve in men's tennis has always been considered the most important shot in the game, we can say that more and more also about women's tennis as their field of play - at all levels - grows to higher levels and deeper talent pools. Any player can compete with great success in today's game by possessing an effective serve, and here in this chapter we will address the ideal technique for this shot.

By covering some elements of technique that many of the best pros in the world each have in common - *the grip, the toss, the shoulder turn, the feet, the throwing motion, and the legs,* we can see how these elements can all work in concert together to establish the ideal service motion, as seen by many of the best pros in the world.

To start this discussion, we must understand that the serve *grip is continental,* or close to it. This grip makes a wide variety of spins, speeds, as well as wrist snap and pronation possible. Other grips such as eastern or semi-western limit one's ability to create various spins and inhibit the wrist movement during contact.

A player's ability to create spin on the serve while using an eastern, semi-wetern, or even a western grip will always be limited. Why would one want to hit spin? Well, just like hitting topspin on a forehand from the baseline, the spin causes the ball to drop into the court, allowing players to hit harder - with more pace - and still be able to keep the ball in. The same is true for the serve. Hitting spin causes the serve to drop faster downward into the court - it basically enhances gravity - and your serves can drop into the service box even when hit with great speed when spin is used effectively. Hitting spin on your serve makes it a more high percentage shot. Most pros will hit almost as much spin as they possibly can hit on their second serves to make it a high percentage shot to avoid double faulting.

Also the spin causes the ball to slide low and to the left on a slice serve (for right-handers), or kick up high and to the right on a kick serve, making for a difficult and often unpredictable chore for a returner to get the serve back into to play to start the point. Using a continental grip makes it natural and easy for players to brush up and across the ball for a kick serve and brush to the side of the ball for a slice serve. This is true because the racquet face naturally faces toward the court when players swing up to hit the ball after tossing it up in the air.

What the some potential consequences of using other grips? Well, with eastern or western grips, the racquet face tends to point far to the right as the server swings up to hit the ball - often even pointing toward the next court off to the right, making it really difficult to brush across or to the side of the ball to hit spin if they are turning their shoulders properly, which will be covered below. These grips can also force players to use more of an open posture with their shoulders to be able to control the shot, taking away one's ability to use their shoulder turn as part of the throwing motion of the serve. We often see players with these grips turning their shoulders very little, or much less than pros do, making the serve more of an all-arm shot. And the more western the grip used is, the more prone to these consequences players can be.

Because the wrong grip can negatively affect the shoulder turn, consequently the contact point will also be compromised. Players who turn their shoulders very little, or less than what the ideal is, as we are describing here in this article, have trouble reaching up as high as they can to reach maximum height to strike the ball. Often a bent arm during a contact point that is too low can be a side effect. So as we can see, having eastern or western grips during the serve can cause a chain reaction of things that can negatively affect your technique, and we will assume that, as we continue to define the elements of the ideal service motion, shoulder turn, wrist action, contact point, and spin are all possible with the foundation of having a continental grip on the serve.

Secondly, we must understand *how to line up with the feet* to start. Typically, for a right handed player, the left foot lines up parallel to the baseline, an inch or so away from the baseline and a foot or two to the side of the middle hash mark. Depending on whether you choose to use *the pinpoint or platform stance* with your feet (to learn more about these two options with weight transfer and feet movement click here - provide link), the right toes will be either a few feet to the right of the left heel, or a few inches. By placing the feet in this position, the server automatically begins in a sideways posture, thus mimicking the start of the shoulder turn that a baseball pitcher uses. Because the serve is so much about the throwing motion, any player will want to develop their throwing motion that includes a good shoulder turn.

In regards to how the feet work throughout the entire service technique, Carlos

Moya and Patrick Rafter are good examples of the pinpoint method, while Roger Federer and Pete Sampras perform the platform method of footwork.

The platform method involves keeping both feet closer to one another and still before jumping up to hit the ball, while the pinpoint method involves starting with the right foot further back behind the left and then dragging it up next to the left before the jump.

As you hold the racquet in your right hand with your continental grip, the best servers in the world hold the ball comfortably in their left hand fingertips, with the palm up. Players that hold the ball in their palm instead of the fingertips lose control of their toss more often because this method lends itself to the likelihood of flipping the wrist to toss the ball up - often with spin - instead of keeping the wrist straight and tossing the ball up with no spin. Holding it in the fingertips gives the player the best chance to lay the ball up in the air in the best place for them.

Both hands begin together held at or a little above waist level, which allows you a good starting point to have a "down together and up together" service motion - where both the right hand with the racquet and the left hand with the ball move downward toward the ground before moving upward together in unison. This is a major aspect of how pros today perform both the execution of the right hand throwing motion to contact and the toss together. While that brief statement may sound familiar, think of it as an overview to which we will now discuss the details of that performing that technique.

Before we delve into the how, of this "down together and up together" method, let's take a look at some of the pros that employ it. Federer, Safin, Davydenko, Agassi, Graf, Navritilova, Gustavo Kuerton, and Andy Murray - just to name a few - all execute their service motions this way - so it's worth considering.

These pros use this method because - when both hands come up together as the player releases the toss up in the air and the right hand holding the racquet moves near the right ear - players have an easier time swinging up after the ball - and an easier time contacting the ball at the highest point to which the player can reach. Hitting the ball it the peak height gives the server a chance to strike the ball at the highest point possible that one can reach - making the player literally as tall as they can be during the shot. We all know taller players have an easier time for the most part than shorter players serving, right? Well, when both hands come up in unison during the motion, reaching up to hit the ball at the peak becomes easier and more natural, than, say, for example, a player who reaches up with his (or her) left hand first during the service motion, and then brings the right hand up much later. The ball toss has more time - because the right hand lags way behind - to drop due to gravity - thus making it more difficult to hit the ball at the peak.

Also, and perhaps just as importantly - the down together and up together method provides players to move through their service motion with a good rhythm. The overall flow and smoothness of movement throughout the service motion is a vital key to generating maximum racquet speed and comfort throughout the shot, and the down together and up together method contributes to this rhythm of achieving one long, constant free-flowing motion with the racquet and arms. Other methods can at times contribute to the stopping of motion at different places in the throwing motion, which decreases one's ability to generate racquet speed, whereas the constant nonstop motion lends itself to creating more racquet speed and consequently more potential to create power and spin.

Certainly one must think of the throwing motion in the serve as similar to how a baseball pitcher throws. In relation to how the right hand (holding the ball) swings back behind the right shoulder before bringing the right hand up near the right ear, the right hand then moves from the right ear upward and slightly to the right over and above the right shoulder as it propels forward to release the ball.

As all of this takes place, the shoulders of a baseball pitcher turn sideways as the right hand reaches back, and the shoulders open up upon releasing the ball with the chest facing the throwing target.

This throwing motion is very useful for tennis players learning the serve. Typically, the better the throwing motion - the better the serve. So when you are learning to serve - or even when you are learning to serve better - throwing around a baseball or football during warm up is a great way to improve your technique.

As we relate the above notions to your serve technique - we must return to how a player lines up in the beginning. So after beginning with both hands and feet as described above, the left hand (which remains with the palm facing upward to the sky holding the ball) falls smoothly downward, touching the inner left thigh before reaching upward and parallel along the baseline to toss the ball. Andy Murray does this to perfection and his shoulder turn is natural and significant.

By reaching along the baseline as one reaches up to toss the ball, players are ensured to have a good (or at least much better) *shoulder turn* during the service motion. By contrast, reaching with the left tossing hand toward the middle line of the service box ensures an open posture that inhibits the shoulder turn, thus compromising power and accuracy due to the restricted shoulder turn (which also negatively affects contact point).

The shoulder turn of the serve is a major part of the service technique, and just after the toss goes up in the air, all of the pros mentioned above that employ this "down together and up together" method turn their shoulder so much that part of the player's back, specifically the right shoulder blade is visible to the returner. This allows the server the chance to really coil up their shoulders and hips to explode up at the ball as they open up - much like a slingshot explodes forward after being pulled back, which generates power. Also, with the shoulders turning in this way, players have a much easier time reaching up high to strike the ball, whereas reaching up high becomes increasingly difficult with more of an open body posture throughout the technique.

While the left hand falls downward toward the inner right thigh, the right hand can move the racquet downward in concert with the left hand moving toward the ground. And as the left hand moves upward and along the baseline - reaching up to toss the ball - *the right hand - holding the racquet with the wrist straight* (not cocked up or bent down) - the right hand can swing the racquet back behind the right hip and up behind the right shoulder.

If the *throwing motion* is executed with the wrist bent downward too much, then the throwing motion can easily be compromised because it's instantly difficult to for the right hand to get near the right ear before propelling the racquet upward to strike the ball. Players that overly bend the right wrist downward too much either reach up too high above the ear or too low below the right ear before swinging upward at the ball, which takes away a substantial amount of racquet speed potential.

The same often occurs when the wrist is cocked up during the throwing motion, but more importantly the racquet face will be facing WAY to the right on contact if the wrist remains cocked up - killing accuracy and control of the shot. Players who do this have to make a last-second adjustment to straighten their wrist - and consequently the racquet face - in order to attempt to control the direction of their serve. Cocking the wrist up can make it more difficult to hit spin in much the same way having an eastern (or worse, semi-western or western) grip does.

As both hands move up near or above the shoulders during the service motion, this is the time when a slight pause can foster greater racquet speed and thus greater spins and power. This *PAUSE*, involves slowing the racquet movement down (not stopping) as the right hand moves from behind the right shoulder toward the right ear before swinging upward to the ball. Steffi Graf had the most dramatic pause of the aforementioned examples of pros that use this down together and up together method, but every player mentioned above possesses this pause. Graf's pause, like the other pros, enabled her to coil up and explode upward to the ball with faster acceleration than if she had otherwise continued her service motion by moving her hands and racquet at the pace pace throughout.

During the pause, the shoulders should, as mentioned before, at the very least, provide a sideways posture for the server. Often many of the best servers in the world will turn their shoulder more than that - Federer - during his pause - turns his shoulders enough to where his back (or right) shoulder blade is visible to his opponent awaiting the ball for the return, as mentioned earlier.

As this unit turn takes place, a good pause also involves the line of the shoulders to tilt, where the back shoulder – or shoulder of the dominant hand – leans down, and the front shoulder stays up high with the tossing arm. This tilt creates a line from shoulder to shoulder that points upward to the sky, which facilitates an upward swing. The front consequently leans into the court as the back shoulder dips down and the front shoulder points up, preparing the body to elastically load before springing upward.

A good pause also includes bending the knees as the racquet slows in momentum before both feet push off the ground. This jump occurs as the player propels the racquet - from the position of having the right hand very near the right ear - upward towards contacting the ball. *The legs* bend during the pause and then spring up as the racquet springs up to hit the ball. Of course the legs springing upward add another major power source to the ideal service motion. After the legs spring upward, the player should land on his or her left foot - so as to further foster a good shoulder turn. Landing on the right foot would cause a player to open up the shoulders to early and consequently hurt one's ability to swing upward at the ball after the toss.

At this point, both hands have moved downward together and upward together as mentioned earlier. The left hand has released the ball (releasing it above shoulder height) - tossing it up a few feet in the air, and the right hand is throwing the racquet at the ball to strike it. Upon contact, the player will either snap the wrist or pronate, depending on the choice to hit a kick or topspin serve, a slice serve, or a flat serve. While the details or wrist movement on contact is an extensive conversation in itself, the above description can act as an overview of how pros with the best serves in the world today operate.

After contact, the player will follow through with the right hand bringing the racquet underneath the left arm - with the right shoulder pointing toward the ground at the end of the follow through. To do this, one must first - upon landing on the left foot - open up the shoulders, facing the chest toward the net. During this follow through, when the player lands on the ground with the left foot - the right leg bends and brings the right heel up to face the sky.

As we can see, the ideal service motion contains a few important elements. From start to finish, the serve mimics a baseball pitcher's shoulder rotation and throwing motion, and includes specific footwork and wrist movement.

A good throwing motion comprised of the "down together and up together" movement of the hands includes a continental grip, a pause, a good shoulder turn, proper footwork, wrist action on contact, and a good follow through. All of these steps in the process are relatively easy to execute, and putting them all together can give you the opportunity to serve big and serve well. With an awareness of each of these elements of technique within the ideal service motion, you too can develop a good rhythm in your service motion, and start to serve like the pros.

Chapter 14.

The Serve: Using Your Feet and Weight Transfer

How the feet are used on the serve often remains an understated element of importance to many players. But executing proper footwork on the serve can foster greater balance before, during, and just after hitting a serve, and can provide, when performed correctly, greater power and control.

For the sake of reader (and writer) convenience, the language used here in this article will reference service footwork for right-handed players. All you lefties out there please be patient and reverse the language from left foot to right foot and so on. Also, if you know any nationally ranked lefty high school girls that want a scholarship, let me know!

If we watch the pros closely, we will see 2 types of footwork dominate the tour. When executed well, these 2 types are equally effective, and a player must choose one type or the other when learning how to serve. It is best to have consistency with footwork on the serve, and by choosing one method or the other and sticking with it, a player will then have a better chance at perfecting that one method and thus having more stability on the serve in general.

Drag and Jump – Pinpoint Stance

The first type of footwork on the serve is a little more commonly seen that the second type, but that doesn't mean it's a better method, just more common. As seen performed by ATP Tour pros like Gustavo Kuerton, Carlos Moya, Mardy Fish, and by Andy Murray as well, this method of footwork involves beginning with the right foot significantly spaced behind the left foot.

Before we begin to describe either of these methods, let's assume that it's understood that before the jump on the serve, the left foot should never move. While their are exceptions to that rule (see Tommy Haas), all the pros we are using as examples in this article to support both types of footwork, as well as 99.9% of other pros that use either of these footwork methods, keep the left foot still before jumping on the serve.

The right foot for these players using the first method starts more than 12 inches behind the left foot, and for some players up to 24 or 36 inches behind the left foot. And as these players begin their service motion and toss the ball up, the right foot slides up to the left foot and pauses directly next to it for a moment. And once this very brief pause occurs, these players will use both right and left toes to push off the ground, jumping up in the air while the racquet swings up to hit the ball. As previously stated, the left foot remains unmoved as the right foot steps or drags up next to it before the jump begins.

As the players toes push off the ground, the player swings up to make contact with the ball, and the feet land on the ground as the player follows through with the racquet after striking the ball with his or her strings.

After the jump, Kuerton, Moya, Fish, Murray, and every other pro that uses this method of serve footwork, lands on their left foot inside the court, bending their right knee so the right heel can finish the landing facing up to the sky. Landing on the left foot with the right knee bent and right heel finishing up fosters a good shoulder turn that enables these players to swing upward to the best of their ability, as well as follow through completely.

While proper shoulder turn on the serve is another conversation to be had than this one, to put it simply, if a player were to land on his or her right foot, overall balance and shoulder turn execution would be compromised. While Boris Becker was the only player perhaps in the history of the game to land on his right foot and also have a good serve, he proved only that there are exceptions to the rule in everything, and copying him in this instance instead of 99.9% of all other pros would be ill advised to say the least.

By starting the right foot further back, and then bringing the right foot up to the left before jumping, players that use this method believe that transferring their weight from the back foot to the front foot is easy and natural, thus generating maximum forward momentum into the court during contact on the serve. However, because the back (right) foot moves, if it were to move in the wrong direction, problems can occur. Some players move the right foot too far to the right of or even past the left foot, which can compromise balance and the shoulder turn, as well causing players to foot fault. This is why it's essential to bring the right foot up next to the left before the jump, just like Fish, Murray, Kuerton, and Moya do.

Lean and Jump – Platform Stance

The second type of footwork, as mentioned before, is seen a little less often in today's game, but is just as effective as the first method. Sampras, Agassi, Federer, and Roddick are all users of this method. Instead of moving the right foot up to the left, like users of the first method do, these players simply begin their stance before serving with both feet closer together. While the space between right and left feet for each of these players vary in distance, the general rule of thumb for this method is begin the service motion with both feet relatively close together in a comfortable way. Roddick seems to have his feet only a few inches apart, while Sampras, Agassi, and Federer maintain slightly more spacing but still far less space between their feet than users of the first type of serve footwork as described above in this article.

Not only does the left foot stay still in this method, but so does the right. Their feet remain motionless, remain on the ground without moving before jumping up in the air as the racquet swings upward to strike the ball.

With the feet beginning closer together, these players transfer their weight not by moving the right foot toward the court like users of the first method, but rather by simply leaning back and forth, keeping their feet still the whole time before jumping up in the air. These players land on their left foot with the right knee bent at or near a ninety degree angle and the right heel facing up - the same way players that use the first type of footwork land.

The landing is the same for both types of serve footwork, and is often ignored by even high-level players. A good landing stabilizes balance not just on the completion of the serve, but also gives greater balance for players to move either toward the net for a serve and volley play or behind the baseline to hit the first groundstroke of the point. Landing on the court with the left foot with the right knee bent and the right heel facing the sky fosters well-timed and complete shoulder rotation.

This second type of footwork on the serve is a bit simpler than the first method, since these players have less going on, literally move less, and therefore have less that can go wrong. They have no chance of their feet inhibiting their shoulder turn or balance when this method is used the right way. However, players that are just learning this method often have more trouble transferring their weight from the back foot to the front foot, and feel like they can't get their weight going into the ball or into the court as well as they want.

Each type of footwork can propel a player's serve into a much more dynamic weapon. As stated above, the overwhelming vast majority of all players on the pro tour use one method or the other. The important thing for players to consider is which method is best for them, and why. There could be a range of reasons from person to person why one type could be more comfortable.

Trial and error is the only way to really get a good idea of which type of serve footwork is best for you, and often players will cite the reason "this just feels better" as why they end up choosing a particular method. That reason is as good as any, and players should not feel an obligation to choose one method over the other. Coaches should be well versed in both methods in order to better assist their students, since using the feet the right way is a vital aspect of this stroke. Without good footwork on the serve, the stroke is incomplete and a player's full potential can never be reached without it. For players that have injuries (both current and past), ailing bodies, and abbreviated flexibility for any reason, I would advise consulting a coach that is well-versed in good footwork for the serve before making a change to your current footwork and serve technique.

Chapter 15.

The Serve – Using the Wrist to Hit Slice, Flat and Kick Serves

While there are a number of elements within the scope of technique on the serve, using the wrist is an important part for us all as we look to master this shot. Of course, before we begin this discussion, we must understand that the scope of this article will only include the use of the wrist on a few different types of serves that the best pros in the world use today. Also, and perhaps more specifically, the wrist movement varies on these serves within the context of the throwing motion that the serve mimics, while players hit slice serves, kick serves, and flat serves.

But what must be said, to be clear, is that this article explores the various types of wrist movement that pros use slightly before, during, and slightly after contacting the ball. This occurs during the throwing motion of the serve, where a player reaches the point of the service motion where he has begun to swing the racquet upward toward the ball as it lays in the air once a player has released the toss. The wrist movement during this brief moment of the serve can determine what type of serve a player intends to hit, and with how much pace or spin.

The elements of technique (specifically the toss, rhythm and weight transfer, the throwing motion, the shoulder turn, using the legs, and how to move the arms in concert with one another) can all work together, in harmony, to foster the ideal that many pros today have achieved.

Having good serve can mean different things to different people, but like all concepts and fundamentals, taking these ideas and making them your own can provide a good foundation for you and any other player to develop their own style when it comes to executing this shot. It's important to consider that, while using these methods can help your ability to serve bigger and more accurately, hitting with purposeful placement and tactical intention can be just as vital to the effectiveness of your serve.

*   *   *   *

1. The Slice Serve

Perhaps the most profound wrist snap in the history of the game was the one performed on the serve of a player named Pete Sampras. Sampras is widely believed to, even compared to players of yesteryear and of today, have had the best serve of all time, and his wrist snap was a significant part of his technique. As he swung up to strike the ball, he would snap his wrist, propelling his racquet face in an effort to hit the top of the ball (while hitting a slice serve).

During this wrist snap on a slice serve, Sampras' strings would strike the ball after the wrist, before contact while swing upward, bends backward (or downward as it looks if you watch the video of him performing it) slightly before quickly bending - or snapping - forward during contact. Sampras' snapped his wrist downward so much that the butt of his racquet would be facing the sky a split second after making contact with the ball - even before his would bring his arm down during his follow through.

By accelerating his wrist up at the ball and while his arm also swung upward, Sampras was able to generate a great deal of power with his serve. The wrist snap in concert with brushing the side of the ball produced not only a heavy serve for opponents to deal with, but one that spun away from the returner.

The terms "setting the wrist" is fairly common among coaches today, as is the term "breaking the wrist". Another good way to think about the wrist snap is to first set the wrist slightly (cock it up - creating a U or V shape via the back of your hand and part of your forearm) and to then break the wrist (straighten the wrist out first and then continue the movement - bending the palm of the hand downward so as to face the ground).

What's important to consider is that, for a slice serve, Sampras would brush the side of the ball in varying degrees depending on how much spin he wanted to hit on a particular slice serve. He would snap his wrist while striking around 2 o'clock (if the ball was a clock) or so - and by brushing the side of the ball in this way he would create a slice - a spin similar to the rotation of a curve ball where the ball curves to the right - and in this case bounces to the right on court. So if you hear a coach or a player taking about hitting the top of the ball on a serve, this is what he or she means (at least when it comes to hitting a slice serve).

Sampras hit, as many pros do, different amounts of spin on his slice serve from time to time. This was done by brushing less of the side of the ball - by striking closer to 1 o'clock on the ball - to create more pace, a serve speeding at higher miles per hour, and with less spin (less slice). He would also strike the ball closer to 3 o'clock - brushing more of the side of the ball, to hit a serve with less pace but more spin - more slice.

So by snapping the wrist in conjunction with brushing the side of the ball, a powerful slice serve can be achieved.

The slice serve performed in this way is possible for him, and for all players, by tossing the ball not only into the court, but also in a location that enables him to make contact between his right shoulder and his right ear. Placing the toss in front of the baseline allows the wrist snap on contact to take place in front of the body - and also, of course, to create forward momentum. Andy Roddick also has a great slice serve, using a significant wrist snap, and he makes contact in the same place.

2. The Kick Serve

The kick serve in today's game is the foundation of all great second serves. There are many women on the pro tour who never developed a good kick serve for whatever reason, but the vast majority of men on the pro tour learned a kick serve at a young age. While many of the men on tour have reached such high levels of confidence on their serves that they hit both a slice and a kick on their second serves, depending on the situation, most players in general hit kick serves for the second serves because the heavy spin on the kick serve not only offers players a serve that is safe (avoiding double faults), but it's also a serve that bounces high and unpredictably off the the side, thus making it difficult to return. And regardless of your playing ability or age, a good kick serve can be developed with the right ideas accompanying you to the practice court.

That being said, the best kick serves in the world are those where the players attempt to create the most amount of spin that they can possibly generate. To do this, of course, requires the most amount of acceleration that a player can possibly generate. Accelerating the arm while swinging up to the ball can give players a certain amount of racquet speed - with some effort, but using the wrist and the arm while swinging up to the ball can give players the opportunity to accelerate toward the ball faster - thus potentially creating more spin.

Using the wrist on the kick serve is not complicated, however it is a vital aspect of maximizing one's potential on this shot. For an extended discussion of the technique in this shot, and a more overall approach to the entirety of the kick serve, please refer to my previous tennis one article entitled "The kick serve".

Within the scope of the throwing motion, a right handed player will bring his right hand up to his right ear before thrusting it upward and forward to strike the ball. When hitting a kick serve, when reaching up to make contact, the server brushes up the back of the ball and also across the ball upon striking it, creating the spin that, while it is similar to topspin, also has some side spin on it as well that forces the ball to bounce up and to the right when landing in the box on the other side of the net (opposite for lefties).

While brushing up and across the ball can be achieved with limited wrist action, players that snap their wrist as they brush up and across the ball have an added power source, which enables enhanced racquet speed. The difference between the wrist snap on the kick serve and the slice serve is relatively simple: instead of snapping the wrist downward and on top of the ball on contact (as described above for a slice serve), the wrist snaps upward on the kick - starting from the bottom of the ball and then accelerating up and across it. To use the clock analogy on the ball, as done so above for the slice, here on the kick the wrist propels the racquet face to begin hitting the ball at the bottom of it and to the side a litte, around 8 o'clock or so, and then the wrist snaps upward and across the ball to around 2 o'clock. The wrist-snap upward and across the ball forces the strings to strike only a small fraction of the ball, thus creating a great deal of spin. If the strings were to strike more of the ball - a larger piece or fraction of the ball - the serve will have more speed but less spin, and players can use this concept to hit kick serves with varying amounts of spin and speed.

One thing that's important to consider about the upward wrist snap during the kick serve, is that the racquet face must - in order facilitate the maximum amount of spin - point relatively toward the court the whole time. Before striking the ball, the wrist cocks backward slightly and then propels forward within the context of all of this. This wrist snap differs significantly from that of the flat serve (i.e. pronation - which will be covered below...), where the racquet face after contact points far to the right (for right handers).

The wrist snap on the kick calls for the the racquet face to point toward the net - both before contact, and after contact (during the follow through) so spin can be generated.

3. The Flat Serve

To hit a flat serve is to hit a serve with virtually no spin by doing two things: snapping the wrist and pro-nating. To simultaneously pro-nate and snap the wrist on contact produces a great deal power. And Roddick does these two things on his flat serve arguably better than anyone in the world - and he uses his wrist snap and pro-nation to create one of the most - if not the most - powerful serves the game has ever seen. Roddick and others hit their flat serves harder than any other of the types of serves they possess in their arsenal, because the pro-nation during impact causes the strings to thrust straight into the upper part of the back of the ball - preventing spin and therefore causing the ball to travel through the air with greater speed. Roddick's pro-nation and wrist snap has striking similarity to the technique used by Sampras on the flat serve, and we can learn, by a brief examination, that their wrist movement through the shot during contact is fairly simple but remarkably effective - and extremely powerful.

To pro-nate is to propel the wrist from an inward facing position before making contact and then to an outward facing position after impact. The racquet face, before making contact, is pointed to the left (for a right hander) as the serve swings upward to strike the ball. And, as the player is about to strike the ball, the wrist opens up, with the palm facing the ball, thus allowing the player to strike the ball with a straight racquet face to as to flatten the serve out and hit without spin. Just after contact though, good pro-nation means to continue this momentum of the wrist in the same direction as it began before contact - moving the palm of the hand to face outward and to the right.

If we look closely at how they strike a flat serve, we can see Roddick and Sampras with their racquet faces facing outward and to the right just after striking the ball to complete their pro-nation.

Here the wrist snap, on the flat serve, is performed the same way as described above on the slice serve, but instead of striking on top of the ball at 1 o'clock, striking the ball at noon or 12 o'clock enables the player to hit flat or without spin. Again the butt of the racquet faces the sky just a moment after making contact as the wrist beds downward. This time though, the wrist bends downward and outward so as to effectively perform the pro-nation at the same time.

Good pro-nation adds a significant amount of power to a flat serve, and the concept of pro-nation is not unique to the sport of tennis alone. Aspiring martial artists and boxers, when learning proper punching technique, perform a similar motion of pro-nating when hitting a training partner or a punching bag.

We can also see both or either of them snapping their wrists downward as they pro-nate, which, as we have already learned, serves as an added power source. With pro-nation already enhancing power a great deal, a wrist snap during pronation while hitting a flat serve can create some amazing power for players that are comfortable using this technique as they contact the ball.

*   *   *   *

As we can see, the way a player can use the wrist just before, during, and just after making contact with the ball on the serve can have some tremendous effects on the success of the shot. With a good wrist snap and the know how to brush the side of the ball, or across it, and possessing the ability to pronate, a player can use the wrist to help them hit a wide range of serves that can be a nightmare for opponents to return. While using the wrist is only 1 aspect with the scope of the technique on the serve, understanding the wrist movement on these 3 different types of serves (slice, kick, and flat) can add another dimension to your serve and ultimately your entire game.

With the serve being the most important shot in the game, having the confidence to not just start - but win points off of your serve can change your perspective on how good you can be. Of course, if your opponent cannot break your serve in a match, his or her chances of beating you are slim.

Chapter 16:

Mixing up your Serves: Thinking like a Baseball Pitcher

I was fortunate. Like many young tennis players, I played a number of different sports growing up. I used to play little league baseball, high school basketball, and intramural football in college (which my college coach forbid, but I did it anyway). And to all the players, both young and older, I encourage them to play other sports to develop themselves into better overall athletes. Playing other sports can help young aspiring tennis players develop their understanding of athletic movement in general, as well as grow their competitive spirit.

I can share with you one example of this from my own experience growing up, when, as a young jock who played catch with mom and dad almost daily, I was put on the mound in my 3rd game ever in little league baseball. I had never pitched before, but the coach said I had a better arm than anyone else on the team and our normal pitcher had the chicken pox, so there was nobody else to fill in.

So, during the game, I pitched my heart out and did…okay. I gave up a few runs and struck out all the people that could not keep up with the speed of my pitches. We won the game, but I was disappointed with giving up a few hits and runs. To this, my coach responded, "Don't be so hard on yourself. We won. You did a great job. And next practice I will teach you how to throw a curve, how to mix up your speeds, and how to mix up locations."

And he did. We worked on a curve ball, which eventually developed into two different pitches: a breaking ball and a slider. Then we worked on changing locations of my fast ball, and then we worked on a change up. By the time our next game came around, my goal was to always keep the batters guessing, and to throw to different places in the box that would give the hitters the most trouble. It was no longer about just throwing hard – it was about throwing smart.

In tennis, the same lesson can be applied to the serve. A player with a good serve will mix up speeds, spins, and locations. A smart player with a good serve will also cater his choices of serves to whom he/she is playing against. This line of thinking can galvanize a player's ability to exploit weaker strokes of his/her opponent, and can also exponentially enhance the effectiveness of one's serve.

To understand how to do this, we must first list the types of serves available to us. In the complete server's toolbox, he/she possesses a slice serve, a flat serve, and a kick serve. Each of these three serves can be hit out wide in the service box (pulling the returner off the court and into the alley), into the body of the returner (where the ball lands in the center of the box), and up the middle (also called "down the T", or hugging the middle service line).

So there are three different types of serves, with three different places each of these serves could be put in the box. That's nine different options for the server right there, and there are an infinite number of other options (theoretically, at least), if one considers the speeds at which any of these three serves shall be hit.

Here's an example of what I'm talking about.

If I have a first serve, and I want to serve out wide to the deuce side, I will probably hit a hard slice, since my right-handed slice spin tails away from the returner, forcing him into the alley. But I can hit that slice 120 mph that lands deep in the box out wide, or I can hit it 100 mph with a little more spin and a sharper angle-landing shorter in the box, or I can hit that serve 90 mph with a lot more spin and pull my opponent as far off the court as possible.

*   *   *   *

Here's another example.

If I have a first serve to the ad side, and I want to serve to my opponent's backhand – I know that I have a number of possibilities. I could kick my opponent out wide with higher mph's, or I could kick them short and wide with more spin, less speed, and sharper angle. I could hit a heavy slice out wide, a hard slice out wide, or either of those two serves instead slicing into the returner's body. I could also hit flat into my opponent's body, or hit flat out wide. All of these serves go my opponent's backhand, but they all can be struck with different amounts of speed and spin, and the locations can also vary.

This example shows how Rafael Nadal has been able to serve with success to Roger Federer's backhand with such frequency. Though in many of their matches Nadal has served as high as 90% of his serves to the Federer backhand, by mixing up speeds, spins, and adjusting locations, Nadal can still keep Federer guessing with the variety of his serve.

*   *   *   *

These options are all viable to me as a server because they all give the returner a different look. The last thing a server wants is to see a returner develop the ability over the course of the match to return your serve with greater frequency and effectiveness. The returner will have a better chance to do this if he sees the same first serve every point, and the same second serve.

Most good players today hit a kick serve for their second serve. But smart servers will mix in kick, topspin, and heavy slice serves for their second serves to keep their opponents guessing. Though all of these options contain a great amount of spin, which good players use often on the second serve to enhance the safety of the shot and up their percentages, the different spins cause different types of bounces. The kick serve is the most widely used choice for the second serve, however, many pros and advanced players will use both slice and topspin serves as well to keep their opponents off balance.

When these different serves, hit with different types of speed and spin that cause different types of bounces are moved around the box to different spots – the list of options for a server grows pretty quickly and the plight of the returner gets darker and more desperate.

Section 3. Tactics and Strategy

Chapter 17.

Categorizing Styles of Play

Aggressive Baseliner	Counterpuncher	All Court Player	Serve and Volleyer

All-Court Player

The best example of this is Pete Sampras. Sampras spent just as much time at net as he did on the baseline. Sampras would follow his serve into the net, and would also stay back on the baseline after his serve. Pistol Pete, like all good all-court players, would look to use his ground strokes to get to the net. He was a threat both from the back court as well as with his volleys, and while this style may not be suitable for everyone, it certainly provides more problems for opponents than any of the other styles, since all court players possess a wider range of options (at least as far as court positioning) with which to hurt their opponents.

The all court player is most comfortable in neutral and offensive positions on court. Because this style demands players to develop every aspect of the game – to be able to be proficient baseliners, proficient vollyers, and proficient in their transition games, players who possess the all court style often have success on all 4 surfaces. While Sampras never won the French Open, he had some great runs to the Semi-Finals and Quarter-Finals, as well as some big time victories on the dirt in Davis Cup. Sampras changed the sport by making it more popular for fans and aspiring junior players to want to excel from both the baseline and at net.

Typically though, clay does prove to be the biggest challenge for all court players. Depending on what player or coach you ask, you may get different reasons why this may be, and certainly it does vary on a case by case basis. However, generally speaking, because the style calls for players that use it to be good at everything, they often don't become great at anything. While Sampras was definitely great at everything, he was an exceptional athlete that many consider the greatest of all time. Most players don't have his competitive spirit or his athleticism, and with the all court style requiring a high demand for proficiency in all areas of the game, it is common to see players with this style to become well rounded players without any area of their games that are developed exceptionally.

Because of this, when all court players are matched up against players that are exceptional from the baseline during clay court events, the slow-bouncing clay court surface gives the advantage to the exceptional baseliner. The longer points, caused by the slow surface which makes it tougher to hit through the court, thus allowing fewer chances to come forward and fewer net opportunities, often makes clay court matches about baseline efficiency. And on clay, most often the player who is better from the baseline usually wins.

On the other side of the coin, all court players excel more naturally on faster surfaces because of their comfort level in coming forward, taking the ball early, hitting through the court, and making their way to the net. On grass, the player who is most comfortable at net usually wins, and on hard courts, the player most comfortable with taking the ball early, hitting through the court, and finishing points at net usually have the advantage.

Sampras' comfort zone coming forward, taking the ball early, and positioning himself at net won him 7 Wimbledons and 5 US Opens, and a couple more grand slam titles down under. The faster surfaces favor all court players because baseliners have less time to get to the ball and therefore a tougher time covering the court.

The Aggressive Baseliner

The aggressive baseliner is a player that possesses powerful ground strokes. This player likes to take the ball early and hit with power, spin, and angles to control the point. He or she prefers to be in control of the point, prefers to be on top of the baseline while striking their shots, pushing their opponents back behind the baseline or into the alleys.

The main objective of the aggressive baseliner is to use their ground-strokes to create short balls that they can attack and finish the point with. The aggressive baseliner is most comfortable in neutral and offensive positions on court.

Andre Agassi was the quintessential aggressive baseliner. Agassi took the ball early off of both the forehand and the backhand, hitting both flat and with heavy topspin at different times, looking to always control the point and run his opponent from side to side. While Agassi made appearances at the net from time to time, he liked to use his powerful ground-strokes to both set up and finish the point.

Because Agassi spent the majority of his time on the baseline, he did have critics of his net game. While he did have relatively good volleys throughout his career, his net game never developed into a weapon that he wanted to use a great deal. Agassi developed a net game that was sufficient for his needs, and this is what up and coming aggressive baseliners should want to aspire to have – a net game that is reliable when needed.

When Agassi was unable to finish a point with his aggressive attacking ground strokes, he was able most of the time to volley well enough to finish points at the net. His use of the swinging topspin volley throughout his career has been copied by nearly every good player that first saw him do it, and Agassi's ability to stand on top of the baseline and be aggressive with both forehand and backhand changed the game for the better, and aided in our sport's evolution (just as Sampras' all court style did).

The same could be said for Agassi's ability to play defense, his transition game, and his slice backhand. These areas of his game were not developed like other players, but they were not central to his identity on court. What Agassi was able to do was develop these areas enough for him to be able to execute them with proficiency, but only in order to support his desire to use his aggressive baseline shots. In other words, he could hit these shots, but it wasn't who he was – it wasn't his game style – to use these shots to win matches.

The Serve and Volleyer

The serve and volley player is a dying breed, given the evolution of the game. Because players today hit with greater speed and spin from both forehand and backhand, it is more difficult than ever to be successful at net.

Not only do serve and volleyers follow their serves into the net on a regular basis – often on both first and second serves, but they also look to follow in their return of serves as often as they can into the net. They feel strongly about putting pressure on their opponents by coming into the net, and they have confidence that by using their net game they can be successful.

Typically the serve and volley player serves well, volleys well, and looks to avoid playing from the baseline because his or her ground strokes are weaker. The serve and volleyer is most comfortable in offensive positions on court.

Defeating the serve and volley player requires hitting a number of successful return of serves, passing shots and lobs. It also requires forcing the serve and volley player to remain behind the baseline, leaving him little choice but to use his weaker ground strokes. This can be challenging at times, depending on the quality of the serve and volley player, since she will constantly look to find ways of taking time away from her opponent by taking ground strokes on the rise to create approach shots and increased appearances at net. Typically, his ability to take the ball early, take time away from the opponent with approach shots and volleys, and the capacity for cutting off angles through sound net coverage, can cause a lot of problems for any opponent.

The Counter-puncher

The counter-puncher is a player who possesses great footwork, foot speed, and patience. He plays mostly from the baseline and uses his ground strokes to hit with consistency. She has no significant desire to control the points and play aggressively, but would prefer to use patience and cunning behind the baseline to frustrate opponents. The counter puncher entices opponents into playing overly aggressive at ill-advised moments by using consistency, and the counter puncher typically lives off of the unforced errors of the opponents.

The counter puncher likes having a target to hit toward when his opponent plays aggressively and/or comes to the net. With great footwork and foot speed, she can track many shots down throughout the course of a point, playing solid defense by giving herself time to recover back to neutral positions during moments where opponents go on the attack.

The counter puncher is most comfortable in neutral positions and defensive positions on court, and thrives on physical endurance and mental stamina.

Establishing identity

While most player fall into one of these categories when it comes to style of play, or close to it, it should be understood that these categories are outlined here as a guide to aid players and coaches in understanding two things. These categories can help in the establishment of an identity on court, in how that person wants to exercise his or her own main strategy – both in how they go about constructing their own shot selection on a regular basis, and how they go about understanding the type of strategy they can employ against their opposition.

Chapter 18.

Finding and Exploiting Weaknesses

Identification Tools

Extreme Grips	Poor Unit Turn	Poor Movement in 1 or more Directions	Footwork Out of Position
Poor Backswing	Late Contact Point	Poor Follow Through	Body Language

"If you know the enemy and know yourself you need not fear the results of a hundred battles," said Sun Tzu in his book, *The Art of War.* "Invincibility lies in the defense; the possibility of victory in the attack." In other words, knowing your own game, your own strengths and weaknesses, and knowing your opponent in this way as well as possible – can open up a world of possibility in reducing your opponent's effectiveness and maximizing your own.

When you walk off the court after a match, the worst thing you can hear is your opponent telling his friends or parents or whoever how great he just played against you. Maybe he just had a great day, maybe he had more sleep than usual, more compliments by pretty people that day, a favor or three done for him prior to the match, or maybe he just woke up on the right side of the bed that day. And then he took it out on you.

Or, perhaps (unfortunately) your opponent's great day on the tennis court was your fault. Perhaps you made him into a better player than how he normally performs. Perhaps your choices, your shot selection, your body language, or even your game style fit perfectly into the strengths of your opponent.

What you must consider before the first point of a match begins, is first the style of play your opponent plans to execute. Is he a counter-puncher? An aggressive baseliner? A serve and volley player? Does he hit flat most of the time? With heavy topspin? With slice?

By understanding the style of play your opponent chooses typically to impose, you will not only have fewer surprises during your match, but you can also begin to look for and find ways of taking your opponent out of his own game style. You may then force him into different styles of play that he may be less comfortable with.

Second, it is imperative that you gain an immediate understanding, whether before the match, during the warm-up, or in the first couple of games in the match, of which ground-stroke your opponent likes to hit more often (backhand or forehand). This may sound obvious, but I've coached (and scolded) pros on both the WTA and ATP Tour that have played entire matches without considering this relatively remedial concept. The last thing you want to do in a baseline rally is hit with regularity to places in the court where your opponent feels comfortable.

The same goes for your opponent's net game - you should take a close look at which side of the net your opponent can or cannot hit with effectiveness (forehand or backhand). That way, if given an option when your opponent rushes the net, you can exploit a weaker volley as opposed to driving a passing shot to your opponent's more reliable side.

There are some general rules to follow in finding and exploiting weaknesses. Let's assume that we all actively understand that it is a given that, when you take court, you have the ability to understand whether your opponent's forehand or backhand is better, and how they volley.

Outside of that, these principles can open up a wide range of possibility for you as you begin to find solutions to the problems players on the other side of the net present.

First, check your opponent's grips. Players with Eastern grips have trouble with high bouncing shots, where they must strike the ball above their shoulders, as do all players who hit with one-handed backhands. On the flip side, players with Western grips have trouble with low balls near their ankles. Examples of this would be Pete Sampras struggling on the high bouncing red clay at Roland Garros, just as former ATP World #1 Juan Carlos Ferrero struggled on the quick, low-bouncing grass at Wimbledon.

If your opponent hits a lot of topspin, prefers the ball up slightly above waist level, and plays with a Western grip, then you should look to find ways of keeping as many of your shots as low as possible. Patrick Rafter, who hit relatively flat from the baseline, who also came to the net a great deal, and used his slice backhand with beautiful effectiveness, had a great deal of success against Jim Courier, who played with an extreme Western grip on both his topspin forehand and backhand. Rafter would slice his backhand early and often during baseline exchanges, and also come to the net as often as possible, sticking his volleys low in the court to take Courier out of his comfort zone.

Second, understand that you must be willing to adjust your shot selection to cater to your opponent's weak spots. If you feel that just playing your game, hitting your shots the way you like to hit, in places you like to place, is good enough to win on a given day, then good for you. But you may be wrong, and even if you are correct, applying pressure to your opponent's weaknesses will make your life much easier, your victories much more one-sided, and your losses far closer in score. The ideal method of setting up your points, no matter who you are playing, is to take your strength - your best shot - straight to your opponent's weakest stroke.

This philosophy calls for your game to be well-rounded, if you constantly look for ways to win, ways of creating the worst version of your opponent, and ways of finding and exploiting weaknesses in your opponent's game. One needs the ability to play defensive against an opponent who hates to play against counter-punchers. One needs the ability to play aggressive, forward-thinking tennis against those who cannot handle pressure well. One needs the ability to go to the net against players who don't hit passing shots or lobs very well. One needs to be able to slice against those with extreme Western grips, hit heavy topspin against players with very Eastern grips, or hit flat and hard against those with poor preparation. And so on.

When I was in high school, my nickname at the Florida academies I played at was Gumby (after the cartoon character who could morph his flimsy body into whatever shape he wanted), because I could change the shape of my game style according to who I was playing against. Because I had the confidence in my game to hit every shot in the book, play any style necessary, I would cater my game style to my opponent's weaknesses. It would be common for parents and coaches who used to scout my matches to see me serve and volley-ing in my first round match and playing clay court tennis in my second round of a tournament, because I had found ways of exploiting different weaknesses in different opponents.

It's essential to look for shots that you hit better than your opponent does, or find match-ups that give you a significant edge. For example, if your opponent has more developed strokes than you do in multiple facets of the game, but you feel strongly that your backhand is better than his, then you should feel confident that you can win the match if you turn every baseline rally into a backhand contest.

This line of thinking can lead to a range of options for you, against a range of opponents, but it must begin with the ideology of: "Winning means finding one thing your opponent cannot do." Of course, most people have more than one weakness, and your life can get easier if you mix up which weakness you exploit from point to point. This ideology starts and finishes with the simple notion that, "it is not how good of a shot you hit that matters - what matters is how much trouble your opponent has with your shot."

Imagine yourself hitting the best shots, struck with excellent technique - they look great, feel great, and land just as deep or wide in the court as you aimed. And now imagine all of those shots struck in a way that your opponent loves to see the most, and located in areas of the court your opponent is most comfortable. All of those great shots you just hit will get you nowhere, and all that effort will be wasted if you are playing into your opponent's strengths.

If your opponent loves to hit forehands from all areas of the court, and has a weaker backhand (e.g. Carlos Moya), then your job is find a range of ways of not allowing your opponent to hit forehands. The easiest way to do this is to serve to the backhand, return to the backhand, and then hit the first groundstroke or first volley to the backhand. When you find your opponent camping out in the backhand corner, hitting inside-out forehands, you can purposely hit wide to their forehand corner which will open up the entire court for you to attack the backhand. Andy Murray used this strategy beautifully against Nadal in this year's US Open. Murray repeatedly throughout nearly every baseline exchange pushed Nadal wide to his forehand side, and this tactic took away Nadal's devastating inside-out forehand, and it also allowed Murray a better opportunity to attack Nadal's backhand.

Likewise, if your opponent loves to come to the net, your job is to keep him on the baseline. This can be done by hitting your ground-strokes during baseline exchanges with slightly less pace, and more net clearance to ensure depth in your shots to pin your prospective net-rusher behind the baseline. You will also discourage your opponent from coming to the net, if, every time he comes in, you choose the following sequence of shots: hit your first passing shot to one side of the court with a conservative pace, with your only intention to dip your shot low at your net-rusher's feet; then, once your opponent pops up that first volley from his shoelaces, then you can hit your passing shot by him to the other, open side of the court. By always dipping the first passing shot low, you will also encourage your opponent to close into the net tighter and tighter, and this will give you an easier opportunity to lob over your opponent. After a few games of passing shots going by, and lobs going over his head, your serve and volley-ing opponent may grow weary of rushing the net, and choose to stay back on the baseline - and suddenly you have taken him out of his comfort zone.

On the other side of the coin, you must be willing to bring your opponent to the net if he is noticeably uncomfortable with his volleys and net coverage. Throwing in a purposely short slice that baits your reluctant opponent to come to the net can often accomplish a lot more than a perfectly-struck shot to your opponent's strength. While drop shots can be riskier (if poorly hit - too high, too deep), the short slice stays low and can be a nightmare for a player that prefers baseline tennis above all else.

One style to look out for - that takes patience and tactical proficiency to defeat - is the counter-puncher, who prefers to play defensive baseline tennis. (I distinguish the counter-puncher from the pusher, who also plays defensive tennis, lives off your errors, but doesn't play or hit better when you give them more pace). The counter-puncher feeds off of your unforced errors, and generally hit their shots with passive intent. The counter-puncher plays better when you give them pace. The harder you hit - the more they like it, and the better they play.

Lleyton Hewitt is a classic example of this. I remember watching Roger Federer beat Hewitt like a drum in consecutive Grand Slam Finals, by lulling Hewitt to sleep with slow, heavy slices, and a wide range of off speed shots before pouncing on a short ball.

Another thing to always look for is how your opponent moves. Does he move better to the right, or to the left? Does he move well or poorly? Hitting drop shots and angles against players with poor foot speed can be safe plays when used at the right times, just as moving a player wide to a side to where he moves slowly can be a smart play.

For example, we know, since we have a good understanding of proper footwork (wink), that when we are pulled wide in the court, we use the open stance on both forehand and two-handed backhands, because using the open stance allows a quicker recovery time. Because we know this, we can look to make sure our opponent does this too. If he does not, we know he will be slower upon recovery to the middle of the court, and we can take advantage of this. Maybe your opponent never took the time to learn an open stance backhand, for example, so you can look to push him wide to his backhand corner on a regular basis. Tendencies like the way your opponent moves are things you should take note of when competing.

Every player has patterns and preferences, and your goal is understand what they are. Your opponent probably likes to hit his serves more in some spots than others, and he probably likes to hit his return of serve a certain way, and so on. Your opponent has a collection of things he likes to do, and your job is take all of those things away from him. Your job is find at least one thing he cannot do - and then make him do it over and over again.

These rules of finding weaknesses start with analyzing your opponent's technique, their style of play, and their strategic tendencies. As you gain a better knowledge of technique, you can pick up more and more flaws in your opponent's strokes. If they don't use enough of their top hand on a two-handed topspin backhand, if they open up their hips on a one-handed backhand, if they make mistakes in their footwork, or if they break their wrist on their volleys - you can exploit it. And by knowing what they like to do, how they like to set up the point, and where they like to hit their shots, you can impose a strategy each and every point that disallows your opponent any chance of doing those things. You can create less effective version of who you are playing against.

Chapter 19.

The Lost Art of the Neutral Ball

We can all appreciate the concept of playing smart tennis. For some of us, that means tactics, for others that means strategy, and for others still, it means staying emotionally under control - and even giving yourself a positive attitude of encouragement while you are playing a match. No matter what level you play at - whether you are a 3.0 adult playing in USTA leagues, or an aspiring professional looking to take your game to the next level - learning how to play smarter tennis will assist your progress exponentially.

The central aspect of playing smart tennis is shot selection - and this article will discuss the most basic level of smart tennis by defining the elements of shot selection. Because there are only three types of shots in the game of tennis - offense, defense, and the lost art of the neutral ball, mastering shot selection can be very easy for anyone. As we will see, all of them are important - but the neutral shot is the central focus of a smart player.

Offense.

This one should be easy for us all to identify with. What do you do on offense? Hit bigger. Simple, right? With racquet and string technology granting players enhanced ability to hit shots with greater pace than ever before, and a large part of younger generations falling in love with highlight reels and flashy shot-making, hitting big from the baseline is very popular.

But when is a player really on offense? When you get a short ball. This is the only time a smart player wants to pick up the pace and go for a bigger shot. And if you disagree with this idea - perhaps you should chart one your own matches and look at your unforced error ratio. (And by the way - hit a drop shot only when you are on offense - but it better be a good one.)

Defense.

When is a player on defense? When you are out of position, off the court, ten feet behind the baseline, standing outside the doubles alley when you strike a ball, or when you are on the run.

I hear people say all the time - people who don't know how to defend - "Oh, that was great hustle - great defense," after watching someone get jolted side to side during a point exchange, as they retrieve a number of shots. But defense doesn't mean running, or retrieving, or diving for balls, or hustling down a million shots in a point. Defense is a situation that calls for a specific type of shot.

So what makes good defensive shot? Any shot that is hit with a slow enough amount of pace, with enough depth, to allow you time to recover back to the middle of the court and therefore neutralize the rally. Sounds a lot like a slow heavy slice or a topspin lob, right? Well, that's because when it comes to defense, those are usually your only two options - and if you don't slow the pace down - you will be running yourself side to side in that point when all that hustle could have been avoided. Hitting too hard hurts you in this situation, and is simply incorrect.

Of course there are exceptions to this rule. But the rule is there for a reason, and it will always help you. There are occasions when you are pulled wide off the court where the only option will be to go for a low percentage winner, like when your opponent is at net, or when you are so far off the court there is no chance for you to recover back to the middle of the court.

The Lost Art of the Neutral Ball.

During a point, if you are not on the run, and you don't have a short ball to attack, then what position are you in? Neutral. This is the time to set up the point - this is the shot(s) where you want to create your short ball to attack. We all want to be on offense all the time - we all want to be in control of the point - and the neutral shot is where it all happens to create the opportunity to attack.

I ask all my new students the same question all the time - "What's the goal of a baseline rally?" They usually say "to win the point", or "to hit a better shot than my opponent", or "to make my opponent miss". These are all nice ideas - but they don't ever yield any real, consistent results. The goal of a baseline rally is to create a short ball. Using the neutral ball to do that is your best bet.

So what is the best neutral shot? We can't be hitting 90% pace (100% being as hard as you can hit) and think we're going to be consistent, and we can't be hitting half pace and think we're going to create a short ball. So if we hit three quarters pace on all of our neutral situations, or 75% speed, and we aim four or five feet over the net, then we not only will be consistent, but we will also be aggressive. This pace allows for controlled aggression.

Now imagine hitting your perfect neutral ball, with three quarters pace. Doing just this is a major step toward controlled aggression, but it's only the first step toward mastering the neutral ball. Each shot must have a specific purpose within the context of the point, and without a purpose, your controlled aggression will do nothing more than keep the rally going. If you really want to create a short ball to attack then you will want to do one of two things with your neutral ball: push your opponent back behind the baseline as far as you can, or push your opponent wide - with an off the court shot or an angle. If a player pushes his opponent back or pushes his opponent wide on every neutral opportunity, his opponent will either give him a lot of short balls to attack or be running a great deal - probably both.

Let's imagine you and I are playing a point, and we have an incredibly long exchange from the baseline - where we each hit a dozen balls. How many of those will you be on the run for? One or two? How many short balls will you get? One or two? So the vast majority of point play lies in this neutral situation. And if you can master the art of the neutral ball, then you are one giant step closer to reaching your potential.

*　　　*　　　*　　　*

Of course, when you are playing a point, there will be shades of gray to the three types of shots in tennis. If you get a ball that is a little shorter - then you should attack a little more. If you are slightly out position and slightly on the run, then you should hit a shot with slightly less pace and slightly more net clearance to give yourself slightly more time to recover to middle of the court. Knowing your own three quarter pace neutral shot makes it easier to take the right amount of speed off your shots in defensive situations - and it also makes it easier to know how much harder you can hit on short balls. With the neutral ball mastered, an inherent scale of proportion will develop in your game - the easier the shot - the more you can go for - and the tougher the shot - the less you go for.

Many baseline drills can become more effective practice when neutral shots are emphasized. Hitting cross courts, doing the Figure-8 drill (you hit cross court and your partner on the other side of the net hits down the line), and even when your coach feeds you side to sides are basic examples of where you can use these exercises to master the neutral shot. I also like to have my students play entire baseline games where the goal is to be as aggressive as possible with one rule: they are not allowed to go for a winner unless they are at net or have a *very* easy approach shot. Because these drills and point situations usually are rooted in establishing consistency, the proper neutral ball will enable you to advance your level of play within the context of the exercises and ultimately as you play matches.

Mastering the neutral ball gives a player a starting point to playing smart tennis, and makes establishing your ideas of how you want to play and what you want to go for in points much more natural. I wish you luck in your quest to being a smarter player, and with these concepts applied, you will be much closer to becoming the best player you can be.

Court Positioning Outline

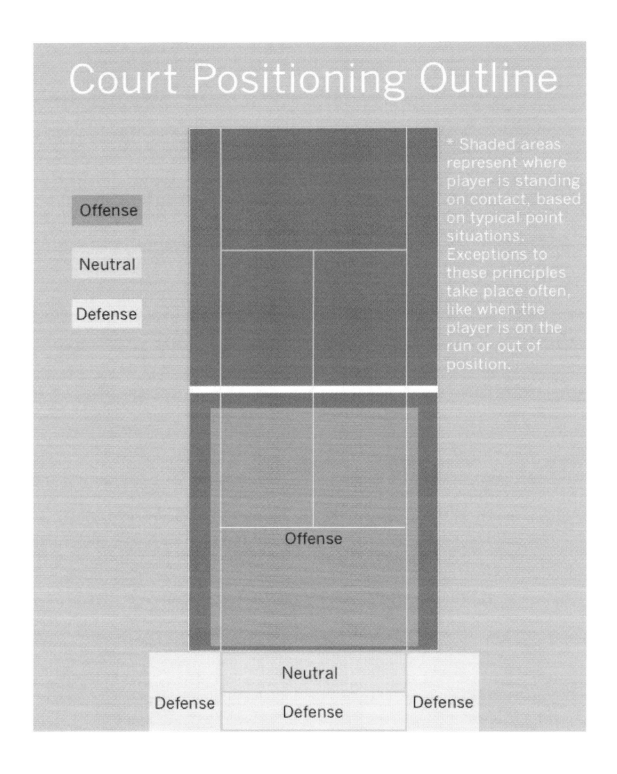

Offense

Neutral

Defense

* Shaded areas represent where player is standing on contact, based on typical point situations. Exceptions to these principles take place often, like when the player is on the run or out of position.

Offense

Neutral

Defense

Defense

Defense

Offense:

Typical Scenario:
When your opponent's shot lands short in the court, with little pace, that you can comfortably make contact at or near waist level without much difficulty.

Choice to Make:
Being on offense is the act of attacking short balls.

Neutral:

Typical Scenario:
When you are not out of position or in trouble in the point, but also when you are not toally yet in control of the point either. Your opponent has not pulled you off the court, you are not on the run - but neither is your opponent. Also neither of you has taken control of the point or received a short, attackable ball yet.

Choice to Make:
The neutral shot is meant to push your opponent off the court in a safe but aggressive way. This can be done in a variety of ways - for example with angles, drop shots, slice, change of pace, etc. However the most common neutral shot used by pros is the 3-quarter pace, hitting 75% speed on your shots (assuming 100% is hitting as hard as you can). The 3-quarter pace allows for safe yet aggressive shots that can easily create short balls if they have good placement.

Defense:

Typical Scenario:
Your opponent has hit a shot that pulls you off the court. You are in some way out of position or on the run, and the shot you are about to hit is a difficult one. Any time you are pulled the court - even if you are in relatively good position for the shot with your feet - you are still on defense.

Choice to Make:
Because you are on the run or off the court, you need to hit a shot that will buy you some time to receover back to the middle of the court and return to a neutral position. Typically, this means hitting a shot with less pace, more net clearance, more shape, and more arc to the shot. The slower traveling ball takes time to travel through the air - which gives you the need time to recover - and the increased net clearance enhances your chances of hitting with depth so as to prevent your opponent from continuing to attack. For example, topspin lobs or slow heavy slices are typical defensive responses, but there are other ways to buy your self time that creativity can allow.

Chapter 20.

Constructing Singles Points

With more and more tennis being played from the baseline these days, it is important for players that spend a great deal of time playing points in practice from the baseline to understand how to construct these points effectively. Ideally, players want to use consistent yet assertive shots to maintain control of the rallies and force opponents into hitting shots they prefer not to hit, while hitting with adequate power in a relatively risk-free manner.

What most players do - even many advanced players - is try to simply hit a good enough shot from the baseline to win the point by creating an error or hitting a winner. This could come from a wide range of possibilities, and often the "good enough shot" that wins the point comes from random shot making. There often is no rhyme or reason as to how these players consistently go about setting up a point, and consequently hitting many good shots over the course of a 2 out of 3 set match can be more than challenging.

But a smart player will use a format - a structure of how to construct baseline rallies for his or her advantage. This structure that we will discuss helps players develop their own patterns of play, their own idiosyncratic sequences of shots that open up the court, hurt their opponents, and put them in winning positions on a regular basis, regardless of the opponent.

This point structure starts and ends with notion of using crosscourt rallies to open up the court. Any player should be aware that when he or she hits a shot crosscourt, the net is lower and the court is longer, thus making the shot a more high percentage play. Players are literally more likely to make their shots when hitting cross-court, so it fosters consistency. When players hit down the line, the court is shorter and the net is higher, thus making for a more difficult shot. Also, because the crosscourt shot is hit at a diagonal, it is easier to create angles that run opponents off the court, into the alley and beyond.

The crosscourt rally is useful for all types of players. Aggressive baseliners, who wish to control the point and run their opponent, can use crosscourt rallies to push their opponent way back behind the baseline or wide into or even past the alley. Counter-punchers can use these concepts in a more conservative way to prevent their opponents from hitting winners by putting their more aggressive opponents out of position, while all-court players can use these ideas to create short balls that they come into the net behind.

Because the act of pushing an opponent back behind the baseline or wide off the court and into the alley can be accomplished in a variety of ways, the cross-court rally is open to interpretation from a wide variety of players and game styles. Using crosscourt rallies is a base concept that players who hit flat, players who hit with slice, with light or heavy topspin, with two hands or one, or players who hit with great pace or with off speed shots can all use.

But the crosscourt rally is only the starting point, so to speak, of this point structure, because players must know when to hit down the line and why. Generally speaking, this point structure lays out some rules - rules that can be broken of course at any time by a player with good cause - but rules nonetheless that exist because they work well for everyone.

The rule states, quite simply, that a player should go cross-court on every shot, with the intention of pushing the opponent back behind the baseline, wide into the alley off the court, for the purpose of forcing the opponent into an uncomfortable position, or with the intention of creating a short ball. During the baseline exchange in a point, *if any one of these things happens, then that is when to go down the line.*

This blanket principle works beyond the most obvious method just mentioned because if a player uses this rule in conjunction with the principles of playing offense, defense, and the right kind of neutral choice (see Chapter 18), then going down the line is a high percentage play when one or more of the four things mentioned above take place.

So, by that rationale, if you push a player wide with a crosscourt angle forehand, then it's a good idea to go down the line with your next forehand, hitting to the other side of the court to further run your opponent. Even if your opponent hits a hard and deep shot back to your forehand, you can move back, play defense by aiming higher over the net and hitting your shot with less pace, and by going down the line in that manner you have not only followed the rules of crosscourt point structure, but also the rules of defensive shot selection.

Another example of that would be if, during a point - in this case during a crosscourt backhand rally - you hit a crosscourt backhand – or your inside out forehand – to your opponent's backhand deep in the court - pushing them significantly back behind the baseline. Even if they hit a decent shot back to you - one that is not a short ball that puts you on offense, but also one that is not a deep or wide ball that puts you in trouble and thus on defense, but rather one in between these two opposite ends of the spectrum - a neutral ball. Because you are in a neutral position, and because your opponent has just been pushed way back behind the baseline, you can hit your three quarter pace neutral shot down the line in this case because, like the first example, you have already put your opponent out of position and off the court through your cross court rally, thus creating a good opportunity to go down the line. If, instead, you chose to not go down the line in this situation, if you chose to go back cross court, you would be hitting your shot right back to your opponent - missing your chance to run them. That is, unless, you choose to hit behind your opponent.

The most effective method of using the cross-court point structure is for a player to use his best shot in a cross-court rally against her opponent's weakest shot. For example, Rafael Nadal uses a great strategy against Roger Federer quite often during their baseline exchanges. Nadal uses his weapon – his lefty forehand – against Federer's weaker side – his backhand. While Federer has an excellent one-handed backhand, this shot for him is least effective when he is forced to contact the ball up high around or above his shoulders. Nadal knows this, and uses his high topspin forehand cross-court to Federer's backhand as often as possible, and thus minimizes the effectiveness of

Federer's attacking style. Nadal often creates short balls he can attack by forcing Federer wide in the court, far behind the baseline, and into uncomfortable positions by using this particular type of cross-court exchange.

The simplest method of using this point structure is to simply hit every shot cross-court during your points until you create a short ball, and then attack the short ball down the line. Once the short ball is attacked down the line, players can make the choice to finish the point at the net or from mid court.

By using these cross court rallies as a guideline to constructing points, you can make your own life out their on the singles court easier, and your opponents' life much tougher. With this concept built into your game as a foundation, you can break the rules if and when appropriate. You will be able to play much more high percentage tennis, and you will be able to establish a disciplined, well-planned attack on your opponent.

Using these rules prevent players from going for winners at random times from behind the baseline, because they know that they don't need to - they know they can hurt their opponents already in a more risk-free manner. They know that all they need to do is use their crosscourt shots to push their opponents back a little, or wide a little to open up the court and thus put their opponents into trouble. They know they can hit down the line after they move their opponents wide or deep cross court, or after they create a short ball, and that by doing this they will always be able to gain an advantage in a baseline rally without taking major risks or going for big shots.

Most importantly, players who believe in this point structure, that use it every time they play, know that if they play their singles points by following the rules of crosscourt rallies, and by following the rules of offense (attack the short ball and take it early), defense (buy yourself time with a shot to allow the chance to recover back to the middle of the court in a neutral or better position), and neutral (see previous chapter as mentioned earlier...).

These rules, when followed promote high percentage, aggressive tennis, and can be a roadmap for both beginners and touring professionals to playing better singles. If a player were to combine the notions of knowing when to hit cross court and down the line – and how (with what pace), with methods of looking for, finding, and exploiting weaknesses in opponents, then a player can begin to play smart, effective tennis.

Chapter 21.

Performing Presence: Demeanor and Thought Processes In between Points

Matches are won and lost often by the attitudes and presence of players in between points, and in between games. When a three and a half hour match at the US Open is played, for example, the actual amount of time spent playing points out is around ten to twelve minutes. So that leaves over three hours during the course of this long match, when the ball is not actually in play, for both players to rest in between points, and to think about what has happened, what is happening, and what is going to happen. That means over ninety percent of a tennis match is spent thinking.

Few players recognize that the overwhelmingly vast majority of time during a tennis match passes not during the points, but in between points. The time in between points is not a down time, but rather a prime time to properly prepare for optimal performance during the upcoming point - and to learn through quick processing - the lessons of previous points.

By focusing on a few key elements, a player can make the most of his time between points. By having an awareness of body language, breathing, energy level, self-talk, the game score, and strategy - a player can consistently walk up to the line prepared and poised to play a good point. All of these concepts can fall into the categories of process or result-oriented thinking, and are often caused by one or the other. Without purposeful use of these fundamentals, a player's presence on court suffers, and consequently so does his performance.

Matches are won and lost often by the attitudes and presence of players in between points, and in between games. When a three and a half hour match at the US Open is played, for example, the actual amount of time spent playing points out is around ten to twelve minutes. So that leaves over three hours during the course of this match, when the ball is not actually in play, for both players to rest in between points, and to think about what has happened, what is happening, and what is going to happen.

Few players recognize that the overwhelmingly vast majority of time during a tennis match passes not during the points, but in between points. The time in between points is not a down time, but rather a prime time to properly prepare for optimal performance during the upcoming point - and to learn through quick processing - the lessons of previous points.

By focusing on a few key elements, a player can make the most of his time between points. By having an awareness of body language, breathing, energy level, self-talk, the game score, and strategy - a player can consistently walk up to the line prepared and poised to play a good point. Without purposeful use of these fundamentals, a player can often lack concentration, poise, tactical intent, and can also let emotions get out of control.

"Our limbs, our faces, our eyes, even our hearts are controlled, at all times, by our brain. We do nothing without our brain and when it comes to nonverbal communications, there is interaction between the mind and the corporal self. Because body language is intimately intertwined with our psyche (what is inside the brain) we can use our corporal behavior to decipher what is going on in our heads as far as comfort and discomfort, thoughts, feelings, and intentions," writes former FBI agent, author, and body language expert Joe Navarro.

In other words, how a player thinks influences body language, and intentional body language can influence thought processes. In between points, when a player droops her shoulders, sinks his head downward, walks slowly with her arms loosely hanging down, and has a grimaced facial expression – there is a high probability of negative self-talk, outcome-oriented thinking, and frustration dominating the forefront of the player's thought patterns. The player is so busy kicking himself that he just lost the last point or game or set or whatever, that she has no time to focus on her energy level leading up to the next point, and also no time to focus on how – with what strategy – she plans to play the next point. This player often loses a number of points due a lack of focus, since he often begins playing points while still aggravated by losing previous points or games, and therefore further contributes to his own demise on court by generating a negative snowball effect that gets worse and worse.

Frustration is often rooted in the desire to win. But what players who get frustrated too often do not focus on enough is the quality of their performance. With process-oriented thinking as the cornerstone to a player's mental output, it is natural for a player with this philosophy to spend time in between points wisely. Because this player is focused on the quality of performance, he knows that he needs to have poise and possess the right amount of energy during each point. She knows that she must regulate her breathing to help her achieve this level of energy and free herself from anxiety. He learns from his mistakes and walks up to the line before each point with a specific tactical intention in mind as to how he wants to play the upcoming point. She keeps her shoulders back, walks with good posture and energy in between points, and keeps her head up at all times. If he speaks aloud, he uses encouraging language, and he has an internal dialogue, he limits it to positive commentary about his abilities and to strategic ploys he plans to execute. She does not worry about the outcome of each point or game or set, she simply concerns herself only with performing at the highest level she can during every point she plays.

"When I savor the moment, a new and powerful source of energy gets released within me," wrote Wimbledon Champion Arthur Ashe in his foreword for *Mental Toughness Training: Achieving Athletic Excellence,* by Dr. James Loehr. "I immediately feel more positive and more in control. Things start flowing automatically. There's no tension, no anxiety, no fear. As soon as I lose this moment, however, as soon as I start thinking about winning and losing, what I should have done or what could happen, all the negatives come charging back."

Players can practice how they walk in between points during matches, what they think about, and how they manage their energy. College volleyball coaches spend as much time during practices cheering each other and huddling in between each point played as they do serving, passing and spiking the ball. This is because the team's preparation in between points has just as much – if not more – to do with their performance, as shot making. The same is true in tennis.

Chapter 22.

Outline of a Great Competitor

When fans sit courtside or on the couch viewing the top pros in the world competing on their television screens, they see players that have risen to the top for a variety of reasons. They see people that possess a range of genuine personal qualities that, together, make them a great competitor. But what, really, does that mean exactly? What specific personality traits and behavior make up a great competitor?

Below is a simple chart that outlines 4 of the main aspects of being a good competitor on the tennis court. This chart brings the intangibles to light, and fleshes out that certain something that some players have, the elusive "it factor" as some people call it, that *je ne se qua*, that ability that some players have who just know what the right thing to do is at the right time on a number of levels, and just simply know how to win.

The 4 aspects are relatively simple, and each aspect as you can see has a number of elements or subcategories within it. Simply put the 4 aspects are the understanding of how to set up a point, the ability to identify and exploit weaknesses, focus, and the belief system.

Understanding of How to Set up a Point	- attack, defend, neutral, - court positioning - give time and take time, - open up the court, create short balls - know when to go to the net - anticipation - use variety to disrupt opponent's rhythm
Identify and Exploit Weaknesses	- grips - technical deficiency ID - poor tactical choice ID - poor temperament ID - poor movement patterns ID
Focus	- play every point with same intensity - ability to problem-solve, fix strokes - ability to change tactics that are not working - ability to play the score - ability to maintain low stress, high poise level

	- process oriented thinking, not result-oriented - energy level ID: self and opponent - body language awareness: self and opponent - match momentum awareness
Belief System	- trust in own strokes - trust in own tactics and strategy - trust in level of play - confidence in clutch moments - positive psychology

Without a doubt, a good competitor understands **how to construct a point**. Knowing what shot to hit and when to hit it is a quality every good competitor has. While different players possess different skill sets, a good competitor uses his skills to attack and defend at the right moments according to his court positioning, and often anticipates what shot his opponent might hit next. Attacking short balls, hitting shots that allow time for recovery when on the run or off the court, and playing high percentage neutral shots to set up the point make for good tactical efficiency.

A good competitor knows how to create short balls by opening up the court and taking the ball early, and also understands how to finish off a point, use variety, and when to implement these ideas. Using angles, different spins and speeds on shots, and different shot patterns to move an opponent are all tools in the proverbial toolkit of a good competitor.

By exercising these skills, a good competitor can more easily anticipate the shot selection patterns of opponents. Also having a good understanding of the parameters of technique and court positioning can facilitate better anticipation as well, as long as the opponent is closely observed.

*   *   *   *

A good competitor always seeks to **gain a strategic advantage**. She constantly looks for weaknesses, has success identifying problem areas in an opponent's technique, shot choices, movement, and temperament, and knows how and when to exploit them.

Watching an opponent's technical aspects of the execution of the hands, unit turn, and movement for each shot can aid in grading an opponent's technique. By taking note of the opponents court positioning and corresponding shot selection, a good competitor will notice choice patterns as well.

Identifying unusual or technically deficient elements in an opponent's unit turn, for example, or racquet preparation with the hands, can create opportunities for a smart player to take advantage of. Seeing a particular pattern of shot choice, as another example, where an opponent goes for a winner when pushed off the court on her forehand side would also be a weakness identification, since the opponent was put on defense but chooses not to play defense and give herself time to recover on a regular basis.

Noticing an opponent's confidence and frustration level in relation to a specific shot can be a pivotal weakness identification tool as well. While some players may look good on one particular shot, reading their face and body language may tell a different, more insecure story. Observing general human behavior in between points, a good competitor will notice what shots an opponent is secure or insecure about.

As Thomas Jefferson once put it, "Nothing gives one person so much advantage over another as to remain always cool and unruffled under all circumstances."

*   *   *   *

Without question, a good competitor has great **focus**. While this can mean many things to many people, the majority of good competitors in the tennis world possess a range of qualities in common that lie within the realm of focus and concentration.

"Our thoughts create our reality – where we put our focus is the direction we tend to go," said best selling self help author Peter McWilliams.

A good competitor plays every point with the same sense of urgency, poise and intensity, and understands that every point matters. Throughout the course of a match, a good competitor maintains a high energy level in a relaxed state regardless of what the score is. That said, he plays the score with purpose and on purpose, using more conservative strategies when down in a game and more aggressive strategies when leading in a game.

She can problem solve, think on her feet, and has multiple strategies planned and ready to implement if and when Plan A does not work. He is obsessed with the process and ignores the result, knowing that executing every detail to the best of his ability will enable him to compete at his highest level on a point-by-point basis, and that is his chief goal. To do this she maintains good, positive body language and posture in between points, walks with a swagger, and observes whether or not her opponent is following suit.

*   *   *   *

Without question, a good competitor has a built in **belief system**. While many outsiders may speculate that this quality is a god-given trait, a good competitor knows that having true confidence comes from putting in the hard work, having the right coaching and guidance, and doing things the right way. A good competitor knows that when the work is put in during practice and training, when the commitment is consistently dedicated to the game mentally and physically, and when an understanding of what it means to be a good competitor is in place, a high level of play is inevitable.

Trusting the work that one has put in, trusting the mentors in a player's life, believing in the tactical, strategic, and technical instincts developed over time – all add up to one simple idea: confidence. Being a confident player means that adversity is just another stop on the train tracks. It means knowing that regardless of the situation, a good competitor can play at a high level regardless of the circumstances – especially in when it really matters.

"Obstacles don't have to stop you. If you run into a wall, don't turn around and give up. Figure out how to climb it, go through it, or work around it," said Michael Jordan, perhaps the greatest basketball player to ever play.

*   *   *   *

Belief, focus, strategy, and knowing how to construct a point are all elements of being a good competitor, and spelling out these intangibles can help anyone become a better competitor on court. The aspects of a player's character on court do not happen overnight, but rather become ingrained within a player's psyche over time through deliberate training. Having good instincts takes time to develop, but by practicing behavior that exemplifies these qualities on court, one can become a great competitor.

Chapter 23.

Wrap Up

There are 26 letters in the alphabet, and those of who speak English fluently can safely say that we have a comprehensive knowledge of the alphabet. None of us really consider that a big deal, but we immersed ourselves in the language, many at an early age, and we did it so much that it became real – and instinctual.

Tennis is no different. With enough deliberate practice, with the 10,000 hours of training as discussed in Chapter 1, with master mentors and coaching, consistent training, ambitious players who are self-reliant, poised, independent, and confident, can find success in this sport. Those players can exceed expectation of small-minded bystanders and reach physical, emotional, and mental potential.

Players who approach tournaments and training as opportunities to learn more about themselves, that understand that life is not happening to them, but rather for them, and that focus more on performance level over outcomes will flourish. They will find joy in the act of playing and they will find more success than otherwise and others who obsess with winning and results. They will be more likely to exert a tremendous work ethic because they are doing more than working toward the chance to win a tournament; they are getting their lives out of the training, out of the playing, and out of the act of the journey. Adversity is embraced as a challenge of the heart, and moving with the natural ebbs and flow of training and matches allows them to operate with awareness and focus.

These players can see things more clearly, and like the alphabet, they know that if they immerse themselves enough, that they, along with the leadership of their mentors, can come to an understanding of every element of technique within their own forehand, and every other stroke for that matter. They understand that with enough training and a genuine interest in how the pros construct points, they will find a deep understanding of offense, defense, and hitting neutral shots to create openings within the point.

These players trust their shots because they believe in the preparation and training that they put in on daily, weekly, monthly, and annual basis, both physically and mentally. Their knowledge of their strokes, of how to play a point, how to combat certain game styles or types of opponents, and identify strengths and weaknesses, along with the deliberate practice they put in gives them the confidence to believe in their own ability to compete and hit their shots through thick and thin, in good times and in difficult or clutch moments.

These players have practiced and experienced their own varying degrees of positive psychology, body language awareness, and energy output, and are fully capable of having awareness of these areas at all times and can manipulate these areas of behavior whenever they feel themselves slipping into unwanted or negative thoughts and behavior. These players have knowledge and training in these areas, and trust their own capacity for finding poise in important moments.

These players understand that biography is not destiny, that personal, psychological, physical, and emotional evolution is always possible, and they welcome change. They understand that attitude is altitude, and that the meaning they ascribe to how they perform and who they are will determine the quality of their humanity on each day of the week, the quality of their achievements minute by minute, their ability to be present moment to moment, and ultimately their happiness and contentment in daily life.

Having these skills are attainable for the inquiring, desiring person. And the off court benefits of achieving such physical and emotional fitness on court are endless. Young junior players who get stuck on their math homework but have been taught these skills on court will be more likely to realize the process of learning the material instead of obsessing with getting the question correct. Adults that adopt these skills will be less likely to expect or obsess with outcomes at work, and will rather find more accidental success in their careers because others will respond to their infectious desire to learn from others and perform at the highest level possible without worrying about how others may judge them.

Having these skills will enhance a player, and these skills will enhance the player's life.

Sources

Freire, P. (1972) *Pedagogy of the Oppressed*, Harmondsworth: Penguin. Classic account of Freire's position. See, also, P. Freire and A. Faundez (1989) *Learning to Question. A pedagogy of liberation*, Geneva: World Council of Churches. Gives an account of learning through problem-posing.

Gagné, R. M. (1985) *The Conditions of Learning* 4e, New York: Holt, Rinehart and Winston. 308 + viii pages. Important study, first published in 1965, that 'attempts to consider the sets of circumstances that obtain when learning occurs, that is, when certain observable changes in human behaviour take place that justify the inference of learning' (p. 5). Basically a systems approach with chapters on varieties of learning (8 types); basic forms of learning (signal, stimulus response); chaining: motor and verbal; concept learning; problem solving; learning structures; the motivation and control of learning; learning decisions.

Jarvis, P. (1987) *Adult Learning in the Social Context*, London: Routledge. 220 pages. Important attempt to ground thinking about adult learning in a sociological perspective. A useful addition to thinking around reflection and experiential learning.

Kolb, D. A. (1984) *Experiential Learning*, Englewood Cliffs, NJ.: Prentice Hall. 256 pages. Learning is approached as a process leading to the production of knowledge. Substantial discussion of the ideas underpinning Kolb's well-known model.

Lave, J. and Wenger, E. (1991) *Situated Learning. Legitimate peripheral participation*, Cambridge: University of Cambridge Press. 138 pages. Significant exploration of learning as participation in communities of practice. Participation moves from the periphery to the 'centre'. Learning is, thus, not seen as the acquisition of knowledge by individuals so much as a process of *social* participation. The nature of the *situation* impacts significantly on the process. Chapters on legitimate peripheral participation; practice, person, social world; specific communities of practice.

Maslow, A. (1968) *Towards a Psychology of Being* 2e, New York: Van Nostrand. In which he argues for the significance of self-actualization. His 'theory of motivation' moves from low to high level needs (physiological, safety, love and belongingness, self-esteem, self-actualization). See, also, A . Maslow (1970) *Motivation and Personality* 2e, New York: Harper and Row. for a full discussion of the model.

Mezirow, J. (1991) *Transformative Dimensions of Learning,* San Francisco: Jossey-Bass. 247 + xix pages. Exploration of some of the processes by which people can free themselves from 'oppressive ideologies, habits of perception, and psychological distractions'. Draws on psycho-analytical, behaviouristic and humanistic theories.

Newman, F. and Holzman, L. (1997) *The End of Knowing. A new developmental way of learning*, London: Routledge. 185 + viii pages. Looks at learning as performed activity.

Piaget, J. (1926) *The Child's Conception of the World*, London: Routledge and Kegan Paul. It is difficult to know which of Piaget's 50 or more books to choose here - but this and *The Origin of Intelligence in Children* are classic starting points. H. E. Gruber and J. J. Voneche (1977) *The Essential Piaget: an interpretative reference and guide*, London is good collection. See, also, M. A. Boden's (1979) *Piaget*, London: Fontana for a succinct introduction.

Retallick, J., Cocklin, B. and Coombe, K. (1998) *Learning Communities in Education, London: Cassell. 248 pages.* Explores the theory and practice of learning communities from an international perspective. Covering primary/elementary, secondary and tertiary levels in a variety of educational contexts, leading researchers discuss: theoretical issues and debate; processes and strategies for creating learning communities; and learning communities in action .

Rogers, A. (2003) *What is the difference? a new critique of adult learning and teaching,* Leicester: NIACE. Very helpful, short discussion that distinguishes between task-conscious or acquisition learning and learning-conscious or formalized learning

Rogers, C. and Freiberg, H. J. (1993) *Freedom to Learn* (3rd edn.), New York: Merrill. Reworking of the classic Carl Rogers text first published in 1969. Looks at how person-centred learning can be used in schooling and other situations and the nature of facilitation. See, also, H. Kirschenbaum and V. L. Henderson (eds.) (1990) *The Carl Rogers Reader*, London: Constable. 526 + xvi pages.

Salomon, G. (ed.). *Distributed Cognitions*, Cambridge: Cambridge University Press. Path-breaking collection of pieces that explore the extent to which learning lies in the resources to which people have access.

Salzberger-Wittenberg, I., Henry, G. and Osborne, E. (1983) *The Emotional Experience of Learning and Teaching*, London: Routledge and Kegan Paul. 155 + xii pages. While largely focused on adult-child interactions, this book demonstrates the power of psychoanalytical insight into a range of learning relationships.

Skinner, B. F. (1973) *Beyond Freedom and Dignity*, London: Penguin. Probably the most accessible entry into Skinner's work and provides a classic account of his all embracing vision of behaviourism.

Wenger, E. (1999) *Communities of Practice. Learning, meaning and identity,* Cambridge: Cambridge University Press. 318 + xv pages. Substantial exploration of situated learning and communities of practice.

Witkin, H. and Goodenough, D. (1981) *Cognitive Styles, Essence and Origins: Field dependence and field independence,* New York: International Universities Press. Account of Witkin's very influential exploration of the impact of context on perceptual judgements.

Dweck, Carol (2007). Mindset: The Psychology of Success. Ballantine Books.

Wooden, John, and Tobin, Jack. They Call me Coach. 2003. McGraw-Hill.

Way of the Champion, 2006. Lynch, Jerry. Tuttle Publishing.

Cox, Richard. Sport Psychology Concepts and Applications, 3rd addition. Brown and Benchmark Publishers. 1994.

Gilbert, Brad. Winning Ugly.

Galloway, Timothy. The Inner Game of Tennis.

What Every Body is Saying. Navarro, Joe. 2008.

Made in the USA
Lexington, KY
05 February 2012